Victory at Yorktown

Victory at Yorktown

By

DONALD BARR CHIDSEY

CROWN PUBLISHERS, INC.

NEW YORK

Library of Congress Catalog Card Number: 62-11816

Printed in the United States of America

Contents

Victory at Yorktown

Chapter One

It was late September, a muggy Monday morning, but from the bumble of thunder and from the rat-gray low sky anybody might have assumed it midsummer, with a storm making up. The wind came from the south, and it was stiff.

Four men sat at breakfast in a two-story mansion at the foot of Sugar Loaf, not far from the east bank of the river a little below West Point. One was a major general, a hero. The others, much younger, might have been his aides, but in fact they were the aides, respectively, of Major General the Marquis de Lafayette, Brigadier General Henry Knox, chief of artillery of the Continental army of the United States, and the commander in chief, George Washington. They were alert, neat, smartly uniformed men, each in his twenties, and they had come to explain that the commander in chief's whole party would appear very soon. They were Major James McHenry,[1] Captain Samuel Shaw, and Lieutenant Colonel Alexander Hamilton.

The plan had been for the commander in chief and his group to stop the previous night at this, the confiscated Robinson residence; but a chance meeting with the French ambassador, De la Luzerne, near Fishkill, had caused Washington to stay there the night. Washington was returning from a conference, his first, with the French generals stationed at Newport, a conference held in a conveniently halfway capital, Hartford, but he was returning not by the way of Danbury, as he had gone, but by a more northerly route. He should arrive at any moment, the famous man. All servants were on tiptoe.

The host general's own aides were Major David Franks and Lieutenant Colonel Richard Varick. There had been a great deal of hard feeling in the "family"—that is, the staff—and neither of those aides was at the table just now. Franks had eaten and hastened away. Varick was ill.

9

The hostess too had sent excuses. Frail at best, she was in bed with her baby.

The general was a rather short man, though heavily built, thirty-nine years old, tough, swarthy, with black hair, ice-blue eyes, and a hawklike face. Nothing about that face changed when a militiaman arrived, saluted, and handed the general a letter, which the general promptly read. But a moment later he rose.

His presence was required across the river, at the fort, he said. Would they please extend his regrets to General Washington and the others? He would be back within an hour, he said.

In truth, he knew that he would never come back.

He hurried off, limping on his right leg. That leg had been wounded twice, and severely, once before Quebec, once at Bemis Heights, the first battle of Saratoga; the general was a prodigious fighter.

He demanded that a horse be saddled and brought around, "any horse." He went upstairs to his wife. He told her, bluntly and swiftly, that the game was up. He must run.

She swooned, that lovely girl-bride, and he left her.

He did not turn north toward the track down to the river. North was the direction of Fishkill, and even in that short stretch of road he might meet the commander in chief. Instead he turned to the right, south. He rode through a gate, across an orchard, through a second gate, into a wood. The ground there dipped abruptly; but the general was a crack horseman. In a few minutes he reached the place where his barge was moored. There were six stout oarsmen, and they took orders, of course, only from him. He jumped in.

There were so many sweet things about the commander in chief that whenever any member of his "family" did wince at an order it was with a feeling of guilt. They all but adored him, those fervent young men, for in the privacy of headquarters, and at mealtimes when there were no distinguished guests, he could lay aside his dignity and tease them and laugh with them like some kindly uncle. They were a palace guard, an elite corps, and they owed it all to the commander in chief, a man they'd work mightily for, a man against whom they would not hear the smallest slur. So loud was this admiration, and so fierce, that there were those who glumly muttered—though only in the right company —that what this new republic really needed was a general, not a damn' demigod.

However, there was one thing about George Washington that none of them ever had got to like, and this was his fondness for early-morning exercise, the indulgence of which fondness, when they were on the road, engulfed all of them. The morning of Monday, September 25, 1780, for instance, he suggested that, instead of having breakfast at the house in Fishkill where they had slept, it would do them all good to ride south and eat breakfast with the Arnolds. The distance was about twelve miles, the road was execrable, and it looked like rain. Yet they loved him so much that they did not groan.

He made it that much worse when, a short distance from the Arnold board (and the charms of the former Peggy Shippen), he announced that he was turning off the road to the right, toward the river, in order to inspect a couple of redoubts directly across from the fort. Somebody, abashed, cried that Mistress Arnold would be expecting them.

The commander in chief laughed.

"I know how you young men are," he said. "I know what you're thinking of. Well, why don't you go on ahead? It's a mission. You can carry our apologies."

This was why the three aides sat in the Robinson house now, wondering what had happened to their host, while the fair one for whose favors they had yearned lay in a dead faint upstairs.

Chapter Two

THE REDOUBTS WERE in poor condition. Nor were they manned.
This puzzled Washington. The new commanding officer of the
district had been so eager for the appointment, so insistent that
his wounds would not let him take a field command—he who
ordinarily could not get enough action!—that Washington had
expected wonders. You *did* expect wonders of Benedict Arnold.
That was the sort of man he was. True, he had been on the job
for scarcely a month; but he was a driver, an officer who got
things done. Moreover, his orders, dictated and in part written
by the commander in chief himself, had been explicit. The need
to strengthen the works at West Point had been stressed. "You
will endeavor to have the Works at West point carried on as
expeditiously as possible . . ." Major General Arnold was enough
of a military man anyway to see this need without having it
pointed out. If the British took West Point they would cut the
infant nation in half, killing it.

It was near noon when the commander in chief with the
greater part of the party at last did reach the Robinson house.[2]
There was no host to greet them, nor any hostess. As the higher
ranking aide, Varick did struggle into a uniform and did make
his bow, but afterward he was obliged to go back to bed. It
had been a hard day for Varick, who besides his fever was suffering from worriment about his boss. Varick had not gone
down to breakfast; and a little after nine the general, who had,
came dashing into Varick's bedroom (which also served as an
office), seized two pistols from a desk drawer, muttered something about being needed over at the fort, and dashed out. Now,
in a similarly unceremonious manner, came the general's lady,
who was in dishabille and looked like an upset ghost. The
former Peggy Shippen then stabbed a finger at poor Varick and
accused him of plotting to have her baby killed. He sat up,
startled. He tried to expostulate with her. Half dressed too, he
even followed her back to her bedroom, where she threw herself

12

across the bed and wailed that he was plotting against the life of her child and that somebody was pressing hot irons upon her head. Varick offered to fetch the general, her husband, but she screamed that the general was not available any longer. "He's gone up there, *up!*" she cried, pointing to the ceiling. Then she burst into tears again.

Meanwhile, downstairs, Washington wasted no time. He expressed himself as not at all offended because he had not been properly received, though members of his staff, always touchy about the commander in chief's dignity, did not feel that way.

Alexander Hamilton, as the commander in chief's military secretary, was to be left behind, in order that he might receive any belated messages. The others would cross the river. Doubtless when they met him over there, General Arnold would explain this apparent rudeness.

They did not meet him over there. There was no salute, no guard of honor—and no Benedict Arnold. Such officers as did greet them were patently flustered, for they had not expected this party.

Washington examined the defenses and was shocked. Next to nothing had been done, except that the garrison had been broken into many small detachments, working parties or sentry parties, scattered over the adjacent countryside, some of them as far away as Fishkill. This stronghold, which it had taken three years to build, at any sudden determined attack would fall like an apple from a tree.

Now more than ever did the commander in chief wish to see General Arnold. His face was grim as he returned to the Robinson house.

Hamilton's face was more than that—it was as pale as death. Hamilton's hand shook when he passed to his chief the papers he held.

A dispatch had come a little while ago from the officer in charge at North Castle, an outpost down the river. Sensing its importance, Hamilton had taken the liberty of opening it.

This dispatch, from Lieutenant Colonel John Jameson, had

been sent at the same time, the previous night, as the one which had so startled Benedict Arnold in this same room a few hours earlier. In usual circumstances the bearer, one Lieutenant Solomon Allen, would have reached the commander in chief some time before the other messenger reached Arnold, for Allen had been exceptionally well mounted. But Allen had not known of the change of route from Hartford, and he had gone direct to Danbury, thinking to intercept the commander in chief there. So it was that George Washington did not get these papers until the middle of the afternoon.

There were six of them. A covering letter from the colonel explained that they had been taken from one John Anderson, a man in civilian attire but with the manner of a soldier, who had been arrested, quite by chance, by some "irregular militiamen" (little better than highway robbers) down in Westchester County. Anderson had been headed toward New York City. Disgusted because his pockets and wallet yielded so little, while his jewelry was made up only of a watch, the Skinners—as the rebel irregulars who infested that thirty-mile no man's land were called—had forced the traveler to strip, and the papers had been found in his stockings.

Several were in General Arnold's own handwriting, which was familiar to General Washington. There were plans of the fort at West Point and of the various outposts, together with an accounting of the artillery and an outline of the appalling weaknesses of the place. There was a copy of the minutes of an extremely important council of war held at headquarters September 6; the commander in chief himself had sent this, confidentially of course, to Benedict Arnold. There was also a let-pass—this too in General Arnold's own hand—made out to John Anderson, who was described as a man engaged on business for the general. The let-pass was dated September 22, three days ago. It had been found in the prisoner's wallet, not in his stocking. Neither of the Arnold aides, Franks and Varick, who would customarily have written such a pass for the general to sign, ever before had seen this one—or heard of any John

Anderson. General Arnold had not been at the Robinson house
that day, the twenty-second. He had been downriver, assumedly
on an inspection trip.

There could be no doubt that here was evidence of the
culmination or near-culmination of a plot to sell out West
Point.

"And now whom can we trust?" Washington asked softly.

There was another paper yet, this one a personal letter addressed to George Washington by the prisoner himself, who
seemingly waxed impatient in durance. He was not John
Anderson at all, but Major John André, adjutant general of the
British army in America, right-hand man of General Sir George
Clinton. He had been trapped, he sheepishly reported, into
"the vile condition of an enemy in disguise within your posts,"
and after a consultation with a personage he was careful not to
name. All a ghastly misunderstanding, sir. General Washington
would see that. André did not use the word "spy" in this letter:
it would have been beneath him. He had been captured well
within Continental lines and while headed for New York City;
he had been in civilian clothes, without insignia, his hat a round
one, not cocked; he wore no sword and carried no identification;
papers of the greatest military significance had been found con-
cealed on his person; and he had been using an assumed name.
But what did these things matter between gentlemen? André
asked permission of the commander in chief to send a letter to
the commander in chief's opposite number in New York City,
Sir George Clinton, and also permission to send for his, André's,
servant, who could bring decent clothes. He clearly assumed
that once these troublesome details had been attended to, Washington would release him.

That was the *tone* of this letter, a genteel one. But Washington had no time to concern himself with tones. The republic
tottered.

This letter from André, astounding in itself, made it crash-
ingly clear that the plot was nearing a head, if it had not
already burst. A personage like Major André, his Majesty's

director of spy activity in the New World, never would have been sent into the lion's mouth to arrange preliminaries. The attack would come soon. Was it already on its way? Were the British coming? The wind still stood from the south, their way.

Washington heard now, for the first time, of General Arnold's curious behavior at breakfast. It was clear what Arnold had done. When he heard of the arrest of "Anderson," complete with papers—which papers were being sent to the commander in chief, who would appear in person at any moment, and who was no fool—Arnold had caused himself to be rowed down to the British armed sloop *Vulture,* mentioned in André's letter as the vehicle by which he had been brought into these parts. *Vulture* was riding at anchor off Verplanck's Point, about twelve miles downriver. Arnold would have claimed a promised reward. Conceivably he might even plan to lead the attack in person.

It was the opinion of everybody else present that not only West Point but also the commander in chief himself was to be seized, that the plot had been so timed. This did not trouble Washington, a man whose nerves were made of steel. He brushed it aside as he might have brushed aside a fly; and he began to issue orders.

Chapter Three

McHENRY AND HAMILTON were told to get pistols and the fastest horses they could find and to ride south as far as Verplanck's, in the faint hope that they might be able to head off Arnold.

Foraging parties, scouting parties, firewood parties, and the like, were called in. The redoubts on the east bank, the two the commander in chief had first inspected, were ordered repaired by soldiers who would at the same time man them, mounting a guard.

The main army lay in camp in and around Tappan, about twenty miles away but across the river. It was alerted, all leaves canceled, all outflung parties called in. Major General Nathanael Greene was ordered to assemble a whole division of the Pennsylvania line, the best troops Washington had just then, and, leaving all baggage behind, to proceed at night by a forced march to King's Ferry, on the west bank of the Hudson, where he would be given further orders. ("Transactions of a most interesting nature and such as will astonish You have just been discovered," the hurried commander in chief wrote.) This would interpose a considerable force between West Point and the British from New York, provided that the British were planning to make their attack an amphibious one, as seemed likely.

The commanding officer of that telling territory between West Point and the city, under the decamped Arnold, was Colonel James Livingston, member of a powerful family. Washington peremptorily recalled him, appointing to the post, as a temporary measure, Colonel John Lamb. Washington was sure that Livingston could clear himself (as in fact Livingston did do), but in this emergency he could take no chances.

The same thing was done—with the same results—in the cases of sundry lesser officers.

It began to look as though the traitor had played this game by himself. But nobody, yet, could be sure.

All of Benedict Arnold's papers and personal effects were impounded and it was ordered that they be closely examined.

Politely, even apologetically, Washington informed Varick and Franks that they must consider themselves under arrest. They handed over the keys to their chests.

Extra provisions were ordered for immediate delivery to the magazines at West Point, also an extra, extraordinary supply of water.

Joshua Hett Smith was ordered arrested and brought in.

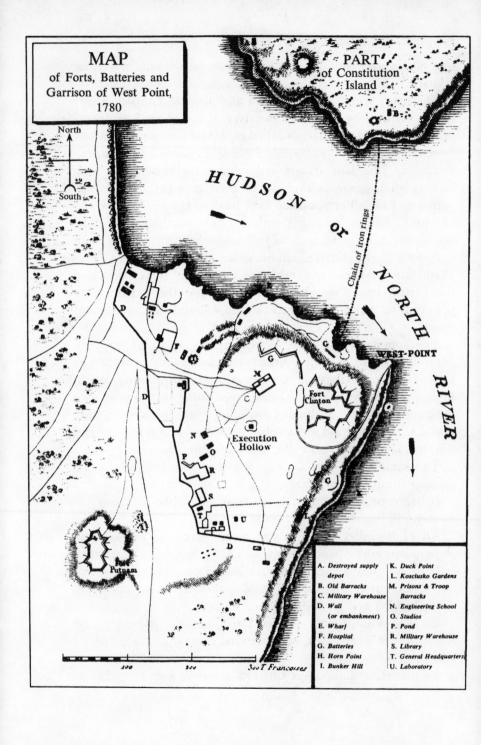

MAP
of Forts, Batteries and Garrison of West Point, 1780

North

South

PART of Constitution Island

B

HUDSON or NORTH RIVER

Chain of iron rings

WEST-POINT

G

G

M

C

Fort Clinton

N

O

P

R

Execution Hollow

G

S

T

U

D

Putnam

100   200   300 T Francoises

A. Destroyed supply depot
B. Old Barracks
C. Military Warehouse
D. Wall (or embankment)
E. Wharf
F. Hospital
G. Batteries
H. Horn Point
I. Bunker Hill

K. Duck Point
L. Kosciusko Gardens
M. Prisons & Troop Barracks
N. Engineering School
O. Studios
P. Pond
R. Military Warehouse
S. Library
T. General Headquarters
U. Laboratory

Franks and Varick never had liked this man, whom they suspected of being a Tory like his brother William Smith, the royal chief justice of New York, and of unduly influencing General Arnold. It was at Smith's house near Haverstraw, on the west bank just below King's Ferry, that Arnold was believed to have spent the unquestionably significant night of September 21-22. It was Smith's coat André had been wearing when caught, Smith's horse he had been astride. Joshua Hett Smith would have a heap of explaining to do.

A message was sent to Lieutenant Colonel Jameson ordering him to send the prisoner to the Robinson house right away. He should be given a heavy guard, so that "he may be less liable to be recaptured by the Enemy, who will make every effort to gain him." Not the usual Crompond route but "some upper road" was suggested, something farther from the British lines. "I would not wish Mr. André to be treated with insult," Washington wrote, "but he does not appear to stand upon the footing of a common prisoner of War and therefore he is not intitled to the usual indulgences they receive, and is to be most closely and narrowly watched."

It had started to rain when at last they sat down to dinner, at the fashionable hour of four.

That was not a cheerful meal. In the middle of it Washington was told that Peggy Shippen Arnold was asking for him, begging for him, upstairs. He went.

She strode back and forth, half-dressed, her hair down her back, sometimes weeping, sometimes screaming, occasionally picking up and hugging her baby. She knew George Washington well—she had thought of him as a family friend, almost as an uncle—but now she stared wildly, while she shook her head. No, no! That was not General Washington! That was some stranger who had come to help Colonel Varick slaughter her baby! He had come to heap more of those excruciating irons on her head, and her husband would be unable to prevent it, since he had gone up . . . up . . . through the ceiling!

Washington left without a word.

Before dark, McHenry and Hamilton, soaked to the skin—for
it was raining torrents now—came back to report. They had been
hopelessly late. Benedict Arnold had been aboard the *Vulture*
for hours before they ever started from Robinson's house. But
—were they *sure* he was there? Oh, yes. He had sent a letter
ashore, by flag of truce. It was addressed to the commander in
chief personally. Here—

ON BOARD THE VULTURE, 25 September, 1780.

SIR:

The heart which is conscious of its own rectitude, cannot
attempt to palliate a step which the world may censure as
wrong; I have ever acted from a principle of love to my country,
since the commencement of the present unhappy contest between Great Britain and the Colonies; the same principle of
love to my country actuates my present conduct, however it may
appear inconsistent to the world, who very seldom judge right
of any man's actions.

I have no favor to ask for myself. I have too often experienced the ingratitude of my country to attempt it; but, from
the known humanity of your Excellency, I am induced to ask
your protection for Mrs. Arnold from every insult and injury
that a mistaken vengeance of my country may expose her to.
It ought to fall only on me; she is as good and as innocent as
an angel, and is incapable of doing wrong. I beg she may be
permitted to return to her friends in Philadelphia, or to come
to me, as she may choose; from your Excellency I have no fears
on her account, but she may suffer from the mistaken fury of
the country.

I have to request that the enclosed letter may be delivered to
Mrs. Arnold, and that she be permitted to write to me.

I have also to ask that my clothes and baggage, which are of
little consequence, may be sent to me; if required, their value
shall be paid in money. I have the honour to be with great
regard and esteem, your Excellency's most obedient humble
servant.

BENEDICT ARNOLD

N.B. In justice to the gentlemen of my family, Colonel Varick
and Major Franks, I think myself in honour bound to declare
that they, as well as Joshua Smith, Esq., (who I know is sus-

pected) are totally ignorant of any transactions of mine, that they had reason to believe were injurious to the public.

That opening phrase, "The heart which is conscious of its own rectitude," was not concocted for the occasion; it was one Benedict Arnold often used. Indeed, the whole letter is characteristic. This traitor, this colossal egotist, always had felt sorry for himself out loud, had bewailed his fate, had charged the rest of the world with plotting against him.

"He wants feeling," George Washington cried.

There were two other letters, also sent ashore from the sloop. One, unexpectedly, was from Beverly Robinson, the very man who had built this house, now a general in the British service. Robinson, it could be guessed, had come upriver with André because he was a ready-made excuse for a flag of truce that might bring André and Arnold together: Robinson could have said that he wished to talk with General Arnold about the storage or upkeep of some of his personal furniture and effects still in the confiscated house. When he learned—from Arnold, of course —of André's arrest and detention, General Robinson wrote, he was shocked. Surely General Washington must know that the adjutant general had been traveling under a flag of truce, had been equipped with a legitimate military pass, and had been on "public business"? Technically polite, in fact this letter was imperious. It treated Washington like an insubordinate servant, all but *demanding* that this brazen wrong be instantly righted. On another evening it might have riled the commander in chief, who had a thin skin for all his hauteur, but tonight he was too busy to care—he had too many orders to get out.

The third letter was the one mentioned in the first. It was sealed and addressed to Peggy Shippen Arnold.

That disheveled witch had recovered from her hysterics and now was merely sobbing. Washington sent the letter to her, unopened, together with word that she might go anywhere she wished on the following day—provided, he might have added, that the British did not attack in the meanwhile.

Troop movements and preparations in that whole section of the Hudson River Valley went on all night, and they worked late too in the Robinson house.

Arnold had originally written in his letter that his wife was "as good and as ignorant as an angel," but he had scratched out the word "ignorant" and substituted "innocent." In this second judgment two ardent young men writing letters in the Robinson house that night—young men tremendously impressed by the Lady Macbeth bedroom act of the afternoon—most fervently concurred. "We are certain that she knows nothing of the plot," Lafayette told the French ambassador. It was to his betrothed, a daughter of the very rich Philip Schuyler, that Lieutenant Colonel Hamilton wrote. "It was the most affecting scene I was ever witness to . . . All the sweetness of beauty, all the loveliness of innocence, all the tenderness of a wife, and all the fondness of a mother showed themselves in her appearance and conduct. We have every reason to believe that she was entirely unacquainted with the plan, and that the first knowledge of it was when Arnold went to tell her he must banish himself from his country and from her forever." Peg was quiet upstairs at that late hour, and no doubt gazed into the darkness with a smile on her small spoiled mouth, pleased with herself that her theatrics had been so effective. And George Washington was writing his report to Congress.

Nevertheless, General Washington was up at sunrise, as usual, for his exercise. They were just bringing in Joshua Hett Smith and the word was that the large party escorting André, a party led by Major Benjamin Tallmadge, was only a short distance down the road. This was good; but what interested the commander in chief even more was the seeming miracle that had been wrought in the weather. As though at a celestial signal, as though it had been waiting for the crack of dawn, the rain ceased, the thunder mumbled itself into silence, and the wind, which had been strong from the south for more than thirty-six hours, abruptly swung around so that it came from the north, blowing downriver.

The British at least would not come *today*, when every hour could be made to count.

Chapter Four

THE WAR WAS NOT going well. The fourth anniversary of the signing of the Declaration of Independence found Washington inwardly perturbed, though he showed serene on the outside, as was his duty. If he could not make some decisive stroke soon, he knew, the whole cause would fall apart. The wonder was that he had held the army together as long as this. The regulars, the Continentals, were hard-bitten veterans by this time, but even hard-bitten veterans can go just so far on empty stomachs. When that spring Washington had sent out a call for 16,500 militiamen and fewer than 6,000 of these had straggled into camp from time to time, even those had to be sent back because there was nothing for them to eat. Of the regulars, by the commander in chief's own estimate, at least one-quarter had no blankets. There was much muttering of mutiny. Many of Washington's own general officers, men upon whom he had been used to rely, for one reason or another, sickness, court martial, death, or just disgust, were dropping out: Philip Schuyler, Charles Lee, Enoch Poor, "Scotch Willie" Maxwell of New Jersey, bluff John Sullivan. The lower officers, lieutenants, captains, majors, who were financially the worst pinched of all, were in dangerously short supply. But if the rank and file went, it seemed almost certain, they would all go at once.

As bad as the lack of clothes and of food was the lack of money. None of the men had been paid up to date, and most of them had not got a dollar for more than a year. This was particularly trying when they compared their own low wages with the bounties that the various states gave, competing against one another, for short-term summer militia enlistments. And when the regulars were paid at all it was in Continental money that never had been much good and now was for all intents and purposes not worth the trouble of picking up: the paper dollar had lately slid from one-twentieth the value of a gold dollar to one-fiftieth, and it plunged with accelerating speed.

Congress, which in its early days, five years ago, had been a noble body, had degenerated as fast as the currency it issued, until now it consisted largely of second- and even third-rate politicians. Everything was left to the states, which by and large were not interested. The commander in chief, scrupulously careful about respecting civil authority and aware of the murmurs of "Cromwell" that swirled in the hall of Congress, made his reports from the field regularly and with exactitude; but when he heard from Congress at all there was a snarl in the sound.

Of the many committees of Congress, the only one in which the commander in chief was directly and immediately interested was that on the conduct of the war, a co-operative body that had worked well with him, representing him and his men before the legislators, expressing their point of view. Suddenly that summer Congress slapped the commander in chief's face by dismissing this committee, which, according to the announcement, had exceeded its authority.

Washington's right-hand man was Major General Nathanael Greene, a large, broad-smiling, slow-spoken ex-blacksmith from Rhode Island, a bookworm who loved to fight and who had been read out of the Society of Friends because of his passion for things military. Toward the end of that terrible winter at Valley Forge two years ago, Greene had been induced to accept the badly bungled post of quartermaster general. This paid well, and he was an expert organizer; but it was glory he sought, it was renown, and, as he himself had put it at the time, who ever heard of a quartermaster general? Ever since that spring he had been striving to get rid of the responsibility and to get some action on the field, a separate command. Perhaps in part because of this—though he was at all times an outspoken man—he had become increasingly gruff and even impolite in his dealings with Congress, where there was talk of accepting his resignation both as quartermaster general *and* as a major general in the Continental army. It might be that even George Washington, the granitic, would have staggered under such a blow.

Fortunately it didn't fall. Congress permitted the rawboned, blunt Rhode Islander to quit his supply post and go back into the line, where Washington promptly appointed him commander of the right wing. (At that same time Washington twice offered the left wing of the army to Benedict Arnold, who, however, his plans maturing, pleaded his wounds and asked yet again for the command at West Point, which was given him.)

The situation in the south was especially serious. As an assistant, Sir Henry Clinton had shown much enterprise and even dash, but, as so often happens, when he succeeded to the supreme command at the retirement of Sir William Howe, he became cautious. For some time after the evacuation of Philadelphia and the battle of Monmouth, he had done little except sit in New York City and call for reinforcements. At the end of that year of '78, he did send an expedition to Savannah, Georgia, a town it easily took. All reports had it that the residents of the Carolinas and Georgia were, if not predominantly loyalist, at least more so than those of the middle states or New England— or Virginia. They would flock in to help, it was believed. They would open their arms and their homes, perhaps even their purses. They'd enlist in droves.

Henry Clinton was a military man, and the idea appealed to him. The original, masterful British strategy had been aimed at cutting the colonies in half along the line of the Hudson River, but this had miscarried with the disaster at Saratoga, and there was little chance just now of another southbound expedition out of Canada. Why not, then, turn the enemy's flank? Strike them in their weakest part? Roll them up colony by colony, starting in the south?

Savannah had been strengthened from East Florida, which Great Britain was holding at that time for no discernible reason, and General Prevost easily beat off a counterattack in October of 1779.[3] In May of the following year, pleased, Clinton himself headed another expedition south, this one for Charleston, which was taken easily enough and with great loss to the Continentals, the surrender of a whole army, including Major General Benjamin Lincoln, whom it was now proposed to exchange for Major General Phillips, captured at Saratoga. Clinton sailed back, but he left behind him a large force led by his second-in-command, Lord Cornwallis, who very soon, and in spite of the resistance of such brilliant guerrillas as Brigadier General Francis ("The Swamp Fox") Marion and Brigadier General Thomas ("Gamecock") Sumter,[4] was marching back and forth across South Carolina almost at will—though he was not picking up many recruits. Soon Cornwallis went a little way into North Carolina as well.

Congress shook its head over the situation in the south, and agreed that a more energetic, more experienced general was needed. The hero of Saratoga, Horatio Gates, had been unemployed, at least in the field, since that event. There were those who whispered that he might do a better job than Washington as commander in chief. Officially General Washington ignored such whispers, which he knew of; but it was no secret that he wasn't overfond of Horatio Gates. Congress, however, *did not even consult* the commander in chief when it appointed Gates to the command of the southern department.

Gates, God knows, was given little enough to fight with; but when he was smashed by Cornwallis at Camden, South Carolina, the news seemed almost too terrible to be true. It ruined Gates' career, for men said that he had ridden away from the field two and a half days before he so much as paused to write a report, and his losses came to almost 2,000 (the British losses: 324), including Baron de Kalb, who was mortally wounded, besides all the Continental guns and baggage.

On the day Washington heard of Gates' appointment—it was June 18, 1780—he also heard that six warships and at least sixty-five other sail had appeared in New York Bay. Those would be Clinton's expected reinforcements, mostly Hessians. Until now the odds had been fairly even, but these Hessians would give Clinton a considerable advantage in manpower and no doubt inspire him to strike—probably north, at West Point. Washington's only chance, as he himself saw it, was if the French, who had promised to come, came.

Shortly after a sad fourth Independence Day, the still imperturbable General Washington heard that three days earlier —that is, July 11—the long-awaited French expedition had appeared off Newport, Rhode Island. It was made up of eight ships of the line—crack ones too, big ones—two frigates, and two bomb-galiots, carrying slightly more than five thousand magnificently equipped troops under Count de Rochambeau.

Soon it became evident that this would not be enough. Besides, the French ships had not brought the promised uniforms and gunpowder, without which Washington could not move far. The British fleet, reinforced yet again and now much larger than the French fleet, took up a position off Gardiners Island to see if the French would come out, something that the French quite properly refused to do.

Negotiations at first were conducted through Lafayette, and they were not very satisfactory, for his own countrymen inclined to look with a leery eye on this young marquis, who seemed to them rash, overeager. For one thing, Lafayette, who was fanatically loyal to his adopted country, again and again asserted that the average Continental soldier was as good as the average European soldier, a manifest absurdity. For another, he thought of his precious George Washington as a divinely inspired miracle worker, an estimate that had yet to be proved.

It was learned that a second French division, with the promised supplies, was at Brest and ready to sail—but the British had bottled it up.

There was still another French fleet, under Guichen, somewhere in the West Indies, and it was hoped that this would soon appear off the coast of North America; but nobody could be sure.

What with one shortage and another, those long summer days, so good for action, slipped away, and little enough was done. It was September 6 before the commander in chief called a council of his general officers on the banks of the Hackensack and submitted to them the plan for an attack on New York, a plan he had already submitted to the French. There were present major generals Greene, Stirling, St. Clair, Howe, Lafayette, and Steuben, and brigadier generals Nixon, Clinton, Knox, Glover, Wayne, Huntington, Stark, Hand, and Irvine, but the commander in chief had promised to send a copy of the minutes of the meeting to the major general who had just taken charge at West Point.

Washington asked for their opinions in writing. These were varied, but most of them were against an attack on New York— Washington's own pet project—unless and until the French had a definite naval superiority, and even more emphatically against a general movement south.

The face-to-face meeting with the French at Hartford did not occur until September 20-21. It was amicable enough, for Washington liked Rochambeau at sight, and Rochambeau liked him. Indeed, all of the French staff officers were charmed with the man of whom they had heard so much: they were fascinated by his impeccable manners. Each commander greeted the other with thirteen guns, and there were many toasts drunk, but there was little else excepting these civilities. In truth, there was not much the two *could* do, Rochambeau's orders and the shortcomings of the Continental army being what they were.

When Washington rode west again it must have been in the lowest of spirits since he had left Mount Vernon six years before.

It was then that he learned of Benedict Arnold's treason.

Chapter Five

Now ONE SIDE had a villain, the other a martyr; and these were equally dangerous.

That pendulous, pudgy, small-minded man who sat on the throne of Great Britain never had been adequate in the role of Mephistopheles. The horns and tail were too big for him, and refused to stay fastened in place. He didn't *look* like a scoundrel, only a fool; and his pronouncements—or what were put forth as his pronouncements—did not *sound* that way. Also, there was the lingering instinct of loyalty, an instinct that five years of warfare had not entirely crushed; for it still was natural for a rebel to say to himself, howsoever quietly, and in the back of his mind, that the King could do no wrong, really. Statues might be toppled, as in New York; but it had never seemed right; and even now it was customary, if conventional, to place all the blame not on royalty itself but on the King's unseen and undoubtedly evil ministers, the men "behind" him. George III just was not good in the part.

Now it was different. After the first moment of near-panic had passed and the first shock had subsided, after each man had ceased to look askance at his neighbor in a terrible split-instant of suspicion, something like relief or even exaltation filled the American breast. For now we really had a villain; and that was a good hard round forceful fact.

In the first place, Benedict Arnold was one of us, and everybody knew how much more bitter were civil wars, how much fiercer family fights. In the second place, Arnold, who whatever else he might lack did have a keen sense of the theatrical, looked like a villain and truly acted like one. There was nothing petty about him, as inevitably there had been about King George. Arnold was a monster, guaranteed; so that the very waverers he had hoped to seduce out of line he instead by his perfidy pushed back.

Almost immediately his name became synonymous with treason, with indeed everything that was hateful and sneaky, so that men on the rebel side soon were saying quite naturally, "Gad, d'ye think I'm an *Arnold?*" and even, "I wouldn't *Arnold* for a thousand pounds!" This effigy fitted. Guy Fawkes always had been a rather remote figure to the American colonists, the Pope remoter still, but Benedict Arnold burned with a bright, bright blaze.

Transplanted, he strutted as before. It had been the belief of Clinton and many of his advisers that the rebel cause was about to collapse, that those in arms on the other side were sick and tired of the whole business and were only looking for an excuse to turn back to their original, their proper allegiance. The royalists, who were thick in New York—voluble too, in the tradition of refugees—had persuaded his Majesty's more formal representatives that Benedict Arnold's defection could prove to be the hole in the dike that might bring about a deluge of common sense. The British, then, greeted him if not warmly, at least earnestly, hopefully. Unabashed, he promised them thousands of deserters—though he did not call them deserters.

His wife, who had spent a little time in Philadelphia posing as a betrayed innocent, soon, bored, asked for and was granted by the rebel headquarters a safe-conduct that enabled her to join Arnold in New York, where society made much of them. They bought clothes. They took a handsome house right next door to that of Sir Henry Clinton himself, which was No. 1 Broadway. They rode about in a coach-and-four, no less. But they did not attract many deserters.

The British made Arnold a brigadier general of the provincial forces, not even of the regular British army, though he insisted that from the beginning—the haggling had been going on at long-distance for almost a year and a half—he had been promised a regular major generalship. They did give him the colonelcy of a regular regiment, which the way the British army was constituted was a minor gold mine in itself. He insisted that the least he had ever agreed to contract for, in cash that is, was £10,000; but £6,000 was the most André had been

authorized to offer him in the event that the plan to seize West
Point miscarried—it would have been much more if the Point
was taken, based in part on a bonus of two guineas a prisoner
—and £6,000 was all that they consented to give him, plus
£315 in expenses. (Benjamin Franklin, when he heard of this
in Paris, cried: "Judas sold only one man, Arnold three million.
Judas got for his one man thirty pieces of silver, Arnold not a
halfpenny a head. A miserable bargainer.")[5]

The martyr was another matter.

As soon as it was certain that no immediate attack would be
launched against West Point, as soon as that stronghold had
been in part shored up and its garrison assembled and strengthened, Washington ordered the prisoner Major André to be
taken to the encampment of the regular Continental army at
Tappan, a village in New York near the river, near the New
Jersey line as well. André was heavily escorted and went by a
roundabout, safe route. At Tappan he was lodged in Mabie's
tavern, where two officers guarded him night and day.

Before this, the protests had started; and indeed André himself was the first to contend that he was no spy, only a pawn.
Yet when he was brought before a military court in the Dutch
church not far from his jail—a court consisting of six major
generals and eight brigadiers, and in the presence too of the
advocate general of the Continental army, John Laurance—the
prisoner had no real defense, and he did not even pretend that
he had come ashore from the sloop *Vulture* under protection
of a flag of truce. This left nothing for the court to do but find
him guilty.

André never ranted, never whined. He was the perfect gentleman, and artistic as well, forsooth. He drew little sketches and
sang little songs, for he had talent—he had written a play, and
it was he who had planned and executed the sensational ex-
travaganza in Philadelphia that marked the departure for Home
of Sir William Howe, André writing the verses himself and
even designing the costumes, female as well as male. At Mabie's
tavern he was permitted visitors, Continental officers who to a

man fell in love with him. A few of these officers, including Alexander Hamilton, even ventured to intervene with Washington in his behalf, vainly.

The commander in chief approved the finding of the court and ordered that the prisoner should die by hanging the following afternoon at five.

Soon afterward the commander in chief suspended this order, for among the many messages he had received was one from Clinton in person which said that the British had additional information and were sending this by a flag of truce. Washington ordered that the distinguished visitors, loyalists from New York, should be received as became their station, but he did not himself greet them; nor had he ever consented to see André.

The British had nothing new to offer, only the argument that André was not a spy since he traveled under a let-pass signed by a major general of the Continental army, and that he ought to be judged only by his intentions, not by his actions.

Washington issued another order, setting the hanging for noon of the next day, October 2.

André had been allowed to send for his servant, who brought him fresh clothes, his full glittering regimentals. Also, André had been allowed to write directly to Sir Henry Clinton, whom he absolved of all blame for his fate, begging him only that he should sell the majority commission for the benefit of the widowed mother and three sisters who would survive—for the family estates in Grenada, West Indies, had lately been seized by the French, and that commission was almost all of the major's estate.

André also wrote directly to George Washington, asking only that his sentence be commuted to death by a firing squad, as became a soldier. Washington had no thought of granting this request—it would have implied to the world that he thought there was something wrong with the conviction in the first place —but he did not reply, thinking it kinder to let the prisoner hope until the end.

The two headquarters were not far apart, and besides the

official flags there had been a great scurrying back and forth on the part of the lesser spies with which both sides were well provided. Thus it was clear that the British were obliquely threatening that if André was hanged, so would be some or even all of the forty residents of Charleston who, after the capture of that South Carolina city, had accepted British protection but had violated their paroles by corresponding with patriots outside the lines. And by the same channels, though in the opposite direction, there went to Clinton the promise—which Washington may never have heard, and which in any case was unofficial—that André would be exchanged if the British were ready to give up Arnold for him.

Nothing came of this frantic exchange of flags, formal and otherwise, despite the circumstance that there appeared to be in the American camp as much desire to save André as could be found in the British camp, where also the lad was greatly beloved.

John André was hanged at noon the next day, according to orders, from a very high gallows erected just outside of the village but within the limits of the American camp. He did not know until the last minute that he wouldn't be shot, and the revelation hurt. But he rallied. He climbed into the wagon and onto the plain pine coffin that had been painted black. Except for the hangman—hideously done up, his face blackened, for he feared reprisals, so great was the prisoner's popularity—André stood there alone. He had politely refused clerical attendance, saying that he was not a believer. He fixed the noose about his own neck, and fastened the handkerchief before his own face, nor did his hands tremble. It was all in the best military tradition, but it was throat-catching just the same. When that slim small young man was turned off, a great wail rose from the multitude that watched, and hundreds sobbed openly.[6]

George Washington, one of the few men in camp who did not attend the execution, must have heard that wail—and must have known what it meant. He was very busy. He was always busy. It could be that he did not even look up.

Within an hour, and while the camp still hummed in anguish, two flag-of-truce messages were handed to Washington, both of them from Benedict Arnold.

In the first, obviously written in the hope that it would reach Tappan before the execution, the traitor blustered typically.

If after this just and candid representation of Major André's case the board of general officers adhere to their former opinion, I shall suppose it dictated by passion and resentment. And if that gentleman should suffer the severity of their sentence, I shall think myself bound by every tie of duty and honour to retaliate on such unhappy persons of your army as may fall within my power—that the respect due to flags [of truce] and the law of nations may be better understood and observed.

I have further to observe that forty of the principal inhabitants of South Carolina have justly forfeited their lives, which have hitherto been spared by the clemency of his Excellency Sir Henry Clinton, [who could not] in justice extend his mercy to them any longer, if Major André suffers; which in all probability will open a scene of blood at which humanity will revolt.

Suffer me to entreat your Excellency, for your own and the honour of humanity, and the love you have of justice, that you suffer not an unjust sentence to touch the life of Major André. But if this warning should be disregarded, and he should suffer, I call heaven and earth to witness that your Excellency will be justly answerable for the torrent of blood that may be spilt in consequence.

Washington filed this.

The second message was a formal resignation of the rank and office of major general in the Continental army. Benedict Arnold wished to keep the record straight.

Chapter Six

"YOU CANNOT CONQUER a map," Pitt had told the House of Commons.

The statement would seem unassailable. After more than five years of struggle, the British held only three coastal cities—important ports, granted, but there were other ports—and such adjacent ports as were needed to protect these against raids. They ruled, that is, the land they stood on; and as soon as they moved, the space was filled with rebels. The whole interior, with its riches, real or potential, belonged to those who had risen in arms.

Yet, who wanted to conquer anybody? This, after all, was a civil war, not an invasion—though admittedly it was a civil war fought with the assistance of British, German, and now French troops.[7] It was by no means a revolt against the mother country on the part of all the inhabitants of all thirteen colonies, or even a notable majority of them. Because of wavering, indecision, intimidation, the refugee problem, and lies, nobody knew or could make an intelligent estimate of the proportion of loyalists to patriots; but this must be large, and especially in the south. The rebels had been better prepared. Conceivably because, as their enemies sneeringly said, they had so little to lose, they had acted swiftly and with decision; and they ruled the roost, inland. All the same, there was many a hidden musket, while many a Tory, openly a patriot, in secret only waited for the word.

Clinton saw this. He was surrounded by the most perfervid sort of loyalists and so he may have been seeing it oversize, viewing the silent ones of the hinterland through a magnifying glass. The war was unpopular, even hated, at home. It was costing a great deal of money while getting nowhere, and there were thousands in Britain who still thought that the hiring of mercenaries was a shameful act. If Clinton could cut the war short, by whatever means, he would be a hero, the more so if he did this without large losses.

Hence Clinton had nibbled eagerly, as in truth he had been duty-bound to do, when Benedict Arnold first approached him a year and a half ago, though at that time Clinton could not be sure *which* major general of the Continental army he was dealing with, so circuitous, so wary, were the unsigned letters he received. Hence he had scorned or pretended to scorn the original, rather meager snippets of information the mysterious applicant sent in, pointing out that they were little better than the intelligence forwarded periodically by his humbler, less highly remunerated spies, pressing that personage who lurked in the shadows to get himself the control of some really good post, some vital place, which could be sold, and *then* to collect a princely bribe.

When the betrayal of West Point failed at the last minute, and Sir Henry found himself without his most valued aide and saddled with a small, bumptious, disagreeable man whose demand for money seemed insatiable—as indeed it was—he could not afford to turn aside in disgust. Whatever he and his associates thought of Arnold personally, *officially* the man was not a traitor from the British point of view, but rather a soldier who had seen the light and had returned to his proper place. As such, and in order to attract others of his kind, they must make a fuss about Benedict Arnold.

It was hoped that Arnold's defection would start a rush to the British lines and so bring about the collapse of an already tottering Continental army. All sorts of inducements were held out, all sorts of noises made. These failed. The rate of desertion on both sides remained about the same; they probably evened themselves out; and in any event, they were negligible.

All unchagrined—for the man had the hide of an elephant—Benedict Arnold wrote in person, directly, to the principal British minister, Lord Germain, giving his lordship expert advice on how to quash the revolt in the American colonies. Some of this was claptrap—"A title offered to General Wash-

ington might not prove unacceptable"—or showed how little
the traitor really knew; but he was on safe ground when he
proposed that the British government offer to any Continental
deserter plenty of food, all his back pay, and, if he enlisted in
the royal forces, seven and a half years of half-pay and a bonus
of from two hundred to ten thousand acres of land, depending
on rank, after hostilities had ceased. Arnold knew conditions in
the camp from whence he had fled. He knew how the soldiers
there suffered.

If you cannot win a war on geography alone, neither can you
win it with only valor. Supplies too are needed. The Continentals had been tried. They were sound, essentially. But they
were hungry, and soon they would again be cold. The fiercest
foe was idleness. Yet it would seem that there was nothing more
to be done that season save retire to winter quarters, a little
farther north than usual, since the army had to be prepared to
protect West Point. It was a dreary prospect, and it damped
their hearts.

Tempers were short. The men were snapping at officers, who
sometimes swore back. Even in higher circles there were scenes.
The invaluable Brigadier General Henry Knox, chief of artillery, a fat and energetic bookseller from Boston, a man with
a pretty wife, a bull-of-Bashan voice, and incalculable deter-
mination, who from the beginning had been one of the commander in chief's most dependable advisers, flew into a fit of
fury, threatening to throw up his commission, when Congress
made Brigadier General Alexander Smallwood a major general,
despite Knox's seniority. Washington quieted him and begged
Congress, privately, to be more discreet about such things in
future.

Washington's own "family," an overworked one at the best
of times, was being whittled. John Laurens had been sent to
France to plead for more men, more supplies, and ships. Tench
Tilghman was in poor health. Alexander Hamilton, who for all
his arrogance was a brilliant staff man, and whose knowledge
of French would be that much the more in demand now that

the French had actually come and now that John Laurens was away, never felt the same toward the commander in chief after the hanging of John André. Nor was Washington's own equability infallible. One morning at headquarters when he had summoned Hamilton he met the aide with: "Colonel Hamilton, you have kept me waiting at the head of the stairs these ten minutes. I must tell you, sir, you treat me with disrespect." Hamilton flared. "I am not conscious of it, sir. But since you have thought it necessary to tell me so, we part." Washington bowed his head a trifle, only a trifle. He did not have a supple spine. "Very well, sir, if it be your choice." Back in his office the commander in chief soon cooled and he sent an aide to Hamilton expressing his high appreciation of Hamilton's services and proposing that the huffy one come upstairs and talk it over. Hamilton replied with a set of written "observations," stilted and rather silly, which said in effect that the lieutenant colonel would stay on the staff if his presence was truly desired but that he would prefer to be transferred to some other duties as soon as convenient.

It was all very unfortunate, and did nothing to improve the atmosphere at headquarters.

Congress had notified Gates that he would be wanted in Philadelphia to face a court of inquiry; and now, in a turnabout, Congress asked the commander in chief if he would "appoint" a successor as head of the southern department, at least until the court of inquiry was finished with its work. All Congressional delegates from the three southernmost states urged Washington to appoint Nathanael Greene, as Washington almost certainly would have done anyway, Greene being the best man. Yet Washington was nice, as always in his treatment of the nonmilitary authority, and he was careful only to consent to "nominate" Greene for the "approval" of Congress, rather than himself "appoint" his friend. Congress did approve. Moreover, Congress put it on the record that Greene should be "subject to the control of the commander in chief." This never before had happened. When a large portion of the Continental soldiery had been operating in the north, for instance, Washington was given no authority over them and in most matters was not even consulted, nor had he had anything to say about the naming of the various southern commanders who preceded Greene—Howe, Lee, Lincoln, Gates. It was a small revolution in itself, and significant. Without any fanfare George Washington had become in fact as well as in name the commander in chief.

Greene got his orders October 22 and started south December 3 with eight hundred horse and one thousand foot, no more than a "flying army." It was hoped that he would be reinforced later, though this was not promised, for the department of the north needed every man it had. Greene was expected to rally whatever was left of the Continental Army in the Carolinas and raise more militia, if possible. Washington assigned to him two of his best officers, Brigadier General Henry ("Light-Horse Harry") Lee and Major General the Baron von Steuben. But nobody was notably optimistic.

Before that, there had been a hopeful note from the south. A group of patriot militiamen, "mountain men," under Sumter, had met about one thousand of the enemy, largely loyalist militia, at King's Mountain—and had sent them running, all baggage and guns abandoned. It was no glorious victory, but it might well discourage loyalist enlistments for a while.

To offset this, however, was the report—undoubtedly correct, since so many spies had forwarded it—that at about the same time General Alexander Leslie had sailed from New York with some twenty-five hundred redcoats, headed, it could be assumed, for Charleston.

Greene would have his hands full. He was greatly outnumbered, and in Cornwallis he was up against one of the best men in the business.

In its new mood of graciousness, Congress passed an army reorganization bill. The changes, mostly a matter of paper, were what the commander in chief had asked for. They would hardly make any immediate improvement, though in half a year

or so, if the war lasted that long, there might be some better-
ment, it was hoped. The principal clauses, in Washington's
thinking, provided that enlistments should be for the duration
and that half-pay should be paid to officers for life after the
war had ended. He had been striving to get these for three years.

Still loath to lapse into inaction, he called another council.
He asked the generals if in their opinion it would be best to
stay where they were, intact, or to send heavy reinforcements to
Greene for the purpose of causing Clinton to weaken his New
York garrison by further shipments south, or to attack New
York.

The council voted overwhelmingly to stay put. And so with
a sigh the boys began to dig in, in a series of camps extending
from West Point to Morristown. They began to chop down
trees and once again to build those huts of dreadful memory.

As for George Washington, he took up what he called his
"dreary station" at New Windsor, New York, where, about
December 15, Martha joined him. She had always tried to be
with him in the winter.

Chapter Seven

THERE WERE THOSE at headquarters and in the various officers'
messes who from time to time, when the inevitable topic was
being discussed, would opine somewhat wistfully that no matter
what his bravado, Benedict Arnold must be suffering inside.
They might have spared themselves the breath. Arnold was a
man whose heart would never be heavy as long as his purse
was; and he was doing well for himself in New York.

October 11 he issued an "Address to the Inhabitants of America," a page full of rant that served no serious purpose save to
confirm, yet again, the nature of the loyalists' propaganda line;

for Arnold in his new quarters was more royal than the King, more Catholic than the Pope.

He excoriated Congress, "the usurpers . . . men who are criminally protracting the war from sinister views . . ." though he had never before found fault with that body, except when it failed to promote him as fast as he thought it should or when it insisted upon investigating the tangled finances of his administration as military governor of Philadelphia.

He said that he had never approved of complete separation and that he was opposed to the Declaration of Independence. He did not add—he didn't need to—that between July 4, 1776, when the Declaration was adopted, and September 25, 1780, when he skipped, he had made no mention of this fact publicly, or, as far as anybody knew, privately, and had continued to draw his pay all that while.

He hammered again a point that the orthodox loyalists loved to hammer (though this was the first time that Benedict Arnold ever had brought it up): That when the royal peace commissioners in the spring of 1778 had offered the colonies everything they asked for save a formal severance from the throne, the offer should have been accepted.

At one time, in the beginning of his long involved dickering with the British command and while he was still governor of Philadelphia, Arnold, always pressed for money, had approached the French ambassador with the offer of his services—if France would pay enough. The offer was turned down, but very gently, politely: it had hardly been enough to account for his flaming Francophobia now, a year and a half later.

For in the "Address" he scalded with vengeful vehemence "the insidious offers of France . . . the enemy of the Protestant faith, and fraudulently avowing an affection for the liberties of mankind while she holds her native sons in vassalage and chains."

Here he touched a telling point. Many an otherwise ardent patriot had his doubts about the Gallic connection. If we had to be tied to some European nation, the muttered argument went, why not at least one that talked the same language? If George III was a tyrant, then what on earth was Louis XVI? Would the French, if we won, benevolently allow us to keep our country to ourselves?

> Can love for you in him take root,
> Who's Cath-o-lic, and absolute?

So the British journals in New York asked, addressing themselves to "the slaves of Congress"—a favorite phrase.

> I'll tell these croakers how he'll treat 'em;
> *Frenchman,* like *storks,* love *frogs*—to eat 'em.

It was crude, but it might have been in part effective, for it was pauseless, persistent, had it but reached the scattered masses beyond the British lines. "The perfidious Gaul" or "the treacherous Gaul" was pictured as a pretty bad person. The Old South Church could become a cathedral, Sam Adams could be made to recant and to attend mass, and no doubt many a shipload of rosaries, prayer books, and indulgences would follow promptly upon the signing of a wicked peace. After all, a real man would stay with his own kind:

> A Briton although he loves bottle and wench,
> Is an honester fellow than parle vous French.[8]

There was a game played on both sides in this war, and it had no name, though it might have been called Stealing Generals. It was an informal game, appealing to those of sporting instincts, for it called for a cool head, daring, imagination. Yet it could have tangible results, rewards; and it was a legitimate if unconventional part of warfare.

The notion still persisted, in some circles, that a leader should lead, literally, in battle as elsewhere. A correctly trained general, or just one with common sense, would stay in the rear, conflict in this last quarter of the eighteenth century being as

complicated as it was; for from the rear—not too *far* in the rear!
—he could survey the whole field, detect signs of wavering in
his own forces or those of the enemy, stop gaps, order up reinforcements, take advantage of unexpected events, sending aides
back and forth with messages, keeping in touch with every
phase of the fray; whereas a man in the thick of the fight could
scarcely be concerned with more than a few score of soldiers
and might have his battle lost right around him while he was
busy giving or parrying blows. Nevertheless, some generals were
so constituted that they had a hard time keeping out of combat,
for they loved the smell of gunpowder, while the whine of lead
was music to their ears, they seeming to have been born for just
this. Such a one Benedict Arnold had been. Such a one was
"Mad Anthony" Wayne. So too, not unexpectedly, was George
Washington ("I heard the bullets whistle," he wrote to his
brother John after his baptism of fire in the French and Indian
War, "and, believe me, there is something charming in the
sound.") It was not unusual in this war for a general to be
killed on the field, as Montgomery was at Quebec, as Mercer
was at Princeton, or to be captured, like Thomas at Trois
Rivières, like Stirling and Sullivan on Long Island, or to become prisoner as part of a mass surrender—Burgoyne and Phillips after Saratoga, Lincoln at Charleston. Netted generals were
not carried through the streets in cages, in the Roman fashion,
but wined and dined and then put up for exchange. A general
—even a brigadier general, who was the equivalent of a whole
clutch of colonels—was a great prize. A major general of course
was wonderful. It took another major general to get *him* back.
He was worth a small battle, just in himself.

Even after the first fright had passed, there were many who
clung to the belief that Benedict Arnold had timed the attempt
on West Point so that George Washington would be captured
along with the stronghold itself. This was nonsense, as the saner
saw. Arnold could not have known far in advance when Washington would come, nor could he possibly have predicted the
wind. Washington, indeed, was the last person in the world

Arnold wanted to see at just that time. Clearly it had been
Arnold's purpose, when attacked according to plan—his own
plan—that he make only a token defense, a show; for he never
lost sight of the agreement that he was to be paid two guineas
a prisoner besides the price of the fort itself. But if Washington
happened to be on hand when the British came, then Washington automatically, as the superior officer, would take command—and there would be a real fight. Nevertheless, large
numbers of patriots continued to believe that the commander
in chief had escaped only by the skin of his teeth, so well de-
veloped by that time was the game.

It could be said to have started with Major General Charles
Lee, who though he came from Virginia was not related to *the*
Lees. He had been a lieutenant colonel in the British army and
at the time of the outbreak of the Revolution had been on half-
pay. When he joined the Continental army, which considered
him a great catch, he of course resigned his British commission.
Charles Lee was a long, sloppy, sardonic, insufferably conceited
man. He was Washington's second-in-command, and would
gladly have reversed those positions, for he had scant respect
for the military ability of the commander in chief, an attitude
he did little to conceal.

Lee was crossing New Jersey with an army to join Washington late in the year of 1776, and was taking his time about it,
ignoring the commander in chief's frantic calls for speed, for
Washington wished to strike some telling blow before winter
closed in completely. The night of December 12, Lee's army
was encamped near Basking Ridge, but the general himself, for
reasons much disputed later on, decided to spend the night at
White's tavern, about three miles outside of the lines. He had
with him a few aides and two unnamed Frenchmen. It was a
raw, cold night, and the official explanation was to be that the
general sought comfort; yet Charles Lee was one of those de-
terminedly rough-and-ready soldiers who often express their
scorn for soft living. The more popular explanation was a
woman. The general indisputably had a fondness for low

women. At any rate, at ten o'clock the next morning, while Lee
was at breakfast with the two Frenchmen, his aides having gone
elsewhere on business, up rode Lieutenant Colonel William
Harcourt,[9] three other officers, and forty mounted redcoats. Out
of Brunswick[10] on a scouting trip, only by chance had they
heard of the general's little picnic, but they took swift advantage of this. They surrounded the inn and called upon him to
give himself up. He did so with amazing, even suspicious alac-
rity, being in a dressing robe and bedroom slippers at the time.
They gave him no chance to dress—after all, they were in an
uncomfortable position themselves—but sat him on a spare
horse and hustled him back to Brunswick. Later he was taken,
dressed, to New York.

Sir William Howe for a little while toyed with the idea of
having Lee hanged as a deserter from the British army, but
decided against this; and the general's durance was not notably
vile.

Retaliation was happy, if a bit late. On the night of July 9-10,
1777, Newport, Rhode Island, being at that time in British
hands, Lieutenant Colonel William Barton, in civilian life a
hatter (the British never could understand how a man in trade
could be an officer, a hatter a colonel, a tanner like Wayne a
brigadier), with thirty-seven officers and men in five small boats
rowed from Warwick Neck, Rhode Island, across Narragansett
Bay, right under the guns of several warships—it was a very
dark night—to a point on the shore of the island about five
miles from the village of Newport itself. Their destination was
a house that stood a little nearer to the village, perhaps four
and a half miles from it, and about three-quarters of a mile
from the shore of the bay. This house belonged to a Mr. Overing, a loyalist sympathizer, and was being used, as being conveniently located between Newport and the British camp on
Windmill Hill, by Major General Richard Prescott, commanding officer of all British and Hessian forces in Rhode Island, to
the number of about five thousand. There was a corporal's
guard in a house about three hundred yards down the road

from the Overing house, and one member of that guard was posted as a sentry at the front door of the mansion. There were also four light dragoons quartered in a house about a hundred yards away, and one of these was stationed in the Overing house tonight: he was asleep in the kitchen.

Barton and his men knew exactly what they meant to do. They were familiar with every foot of this ground. The sentry saw them and challenged twice, but he could not shoot off his musket because it wasn't loaded. He was easily overcome, and the door battered in, and the general hauled out of bed. This took place at just about midnight. There was enough noise to awaken the dragoon in the kitchen, and he ran to the guard-house, but something about that building—actually none of the patriots had approached it—made him think that it had already fallen to the enemy; so he ran back. A Negro servant told him what had happened, and he sprang on his horse and rode off to give the alarm. Meanwhile the general's aide-de-camp, Lieutenant Barrington, with great presence of mind had jumped out of a window; but they jumped after him and captured him, clad as he was only in a shirt and breeches—nor did they give him a chance to put on more. The general himself was permitted to dress, all except for one stocking, which nobody could seem to find. General, aide, and sentry—all were taken, all vanished.[11]

Prescott and Lee were exchanged, much to the vexation of Lee, who thought that he rated a more exalted swap—Burgoyne, say. Prescott, after all, had only lately been raised from a briga-diership.

These events may have been in the mind of Light-Horse Harry Lee when he questioned one of his sergeants major, John Champe, who had volunteered in that autumn of 1780 to go into New York City and kidnap Benedict Arnold. Champe, a tall young fellow with damn-you eyes, a Virginian, was accepted. The plan was for him to pretend that he had deserted and to accost Arnold in the street, offering to sign up with the British. Washington had informally agreed to this, though with the stipulation that there should be no murder. He wanted Arnold, but he wanted him alive.

The thing went off swimmingly at first. Arnold was delighted to get a new recruit for his pitifully thin ranks of deserters from the Continental army, scarcely forty in number, and Champe soon took one or two others into the plot. Champe followed the general, studying his habits, and noted in particular that it was Arnold's custom, each night when he came home to 3 Broadway, to take a stroll in the garden before turning in. Arnold would always be alone at that time, and Champe surreptitiously removed and loosely replaced a couple of the fence pickets. A boat was obtained, to row the traitor across to New Jersey and the Continental lines. Everything was ready. If anybody intercepted them between garden and boat they would say that they were carrying a drunken man to the guardhouse. Arnold himself, knocked on the head, would say nothing.

Suddenly Champe was ordered aboard a transport, and so were his friends and co-conspirators, and after a few days, along with many other transports, and a few warships, they sailed south. Benedict Arnold was on one of those warships, commanding officer of an expedition of some 1,200 horse and foot with instructions to do all the damage he could in Virginia, thus making it harder for Greene to operate against Cornwallis, since all of Greene's supplies came from or through the Old Dominion. And that was the end of that. Champe re-deserted when they reached Virginia, and in time he got back into his own outfit; but he never was close to Benedict Arnold again.

A few nights after that sailing—it was Christmas—another kidnaping party sallied forth from Nyack, New York, in a barge and two whaleboats. There were four officers and twenty-odd men, and they were armed with axes and crowbars. The leader was one of Washington's aides, a poet, Lieutenant Colonel David Humphreys. Their orders were simple. They were to go to Manhattan and under cover of darkness break into either Morris's house[12] in the northern part of the island or the mansion at No. 1 Broadway. In the one case they would seize and carry off General Wilhelm von Knyphausen, head of the Hessians in America and Clinton's second-in-command in New York, in the other of course Sir Henry Clinton himself. The plan was beautifully bold. It did not work. The wind was hard from the north, and became stiffer, so that they were blown past the whole island of Manhattan, without getting a chance to put in safely anywhere, and out past the Battery to the lower bay. One of the boats was driven ashore on Staten Island, all of which was held by the British, but it pushed out again before its presence was noted. They could not put back. They made their way across Raritan Bay to the Raritan River and up that river to a place of safety, and they returned to camp on foot, arriving there New Year's Day.

Thus 1780 closed with yet another failure. And 1781 was to open with a mutiny.

Chapter Eight

MUTINY WAS NOT NEW in the Continental army, but until New Year's Day of 1781 it had come in touches, mere cat's-paws, not engulfing waves. Winter quarters always were horrible, and as much as could be the officers kept the men more or less busy, and warm, by constructing unneeded works—a bridge across the Schuylkill at Valley Forge, a wooden fortress, "Fort Nonsense," at Morristown; but it was touch and go all the while, and breaths were held.

One night at Valley Forge the soldiers in their huts for several hours had catcalled and shouted taunts to the officers, who patrolled the camp streets with loaded pistols, expecting the worst; but nothing came of this.

At Danbury, Connecticut, in the middle of January, 1779, some of the men of Jedediah Huntington's brigade kicked up a fuss, but they were quieted by their officers without violence and before the British, always on the alert to take advantage of such a situation, could do anything about it.

The previous New Year's Day—that is, January 1, 1780— one hundred Massachusetts men, who claimed that their terms of enlistment had run out, started to march away from West Point, and it was only with difficulty that they were restrained; but again there was no violence.

In June of that year, thirty-one New York men marched out of Fort Schuyler, determined, they said, to go home. These too were talked out of it.

Two whole Connecticut regiments of the line had drawn themselves up in parade formation, without officers but with drums and colors and all the rest of it, at Morristown, May 25, 1780. They too were going home. They too were dissuaded, though it took all day.

The January 1, 1781, outbreak was more serious than any of these. It was utterly unexpected; and it seemed for a while about to prove contagious.

The men had legitimate grievances. Half starved, always cold, they did not complain of their equipment and not often of the discipline, their officers; but they did want their back pay and they did ask to go home.

In the case of the six regiments of the Pennsylvania line, encamped at Mount Kemble, near Morristown, the grievances were even more pronounced. Many of these men were foreigners, recently arrived, Germans and Irish. Most of them had been enlisted "for three years or during the war." The three years being up, they asked to be paid and allowed to leave. A military court decided against them and said that they had to remain in the army until the end of the war. That was too much.

The thing flared suddenly, at night. There had been an extra rum ration that day, it being the first of the year, and no doubt a certain amount of this was diverted. The mutiny did in fact have the air of a drunken brawl at first. The men marched in the streets between the huts, shouting that they were going to

Philadelphia and demand of Congress their back pay and their release. They had muskets, and some of them fired these wildly into the air. They had bayonets, and some of them used these upon officers who sought to shoo them back into their huts, so that one officer was killed and two were wounded.

As soon as the officers had withdrawn, however, the men behaved well enough. Their sergeants acted as officers, as though by prearrangement, and they maintained excellent order. A little after midnight, cannons and all, they marched out of camp, keeping careful step. There might have been 1,400 or 1,500 of them, though more were coming in all the time. They claimed that they had 2,000. They drew rations for 2,000.

These men after a few hours stopped and bivouacked at Vealtown. The next day, still quiet, still orderly, they went as far as Middlebrook. And the day after that, January 3, they went to Princeton, where they pitched their tents, making Nassau Hall, the College of New Jersey administration building, their headquarters.

Their officers, with three notable exceptions, followed them as far as Middlebrook, and there they squatted, fretting.

The three exceptions were the commanding officer of the Pennsylvania line—after Major General Arthur St. Clair, who was absent, his wife being sick—and two colonels, Walter Stewart and Richard Butler. The commanding officer was Anthony Wayne, a brigadier. It is remarkable that both colonels were Irish-born. The Eleventh Regiment in which the trouble had started, was largely Irish.

These three went along with the mutineers on their march. They were not mistreated, yet neither were they fawned upon. Nobody, least of all themselves, knew whether they were prisoners or guests.

The Marquis de Lafayette, who happened to be passing that way, going from Philadelphia back to headquarters, asked for permission to address the men. This was refused, and the refusal hurt the Frenchman's feelings. He had been confident that he could speech the men into returning to camp. He had

an almost fanatical faith in the American soldier, and believed
that the present uprising was the work of foreigners and would
not have happened in an all-native outfit.

They went right on conducting themselves well, keeping the
same discipline, for the corporals were acting as sergeants while
the sergeants acted as officers. There was no looting, there were
no insults.

So efficient were Clinton's spies that British headquarters got
the news at the same time as Washington did at New Windsor.
Washington first planned to go to Princeton in person, but after
some thought he decided that his presence was more needed in
the north, in case the mutiny spread to the New England troops
with which he was surrounded. Clinton, on the other hand,
went into instant action. This was his opportunity. He ordered
the sloop *Neptune* to stand by in Raritan Bay and ordered the
sloop *Vulture*, André's *Vulture*, down the river and into that
bay. Though it was a day of teeming rain in New York, January
3, he alerted the British grenadiers, the British light infantry,
the Forty-second and Thirty-seventh Regiments, the Hessian
grenadiers, and the Hessian Jägers, and sent them over to Staten
Island, that convenient jumping-off place for any invasion of
New Jersey. There, however, he held them. The men, all crack
troops, had been directed to have extra shirts and stockings and
each carried three days' rations. There was nothing to prevent
them from crossing the unfortified, narrow Kill van Kull into
Elizabethtown and from thence proceeding to Princeton, where
they could have surrounded and easily captured the mutineers.
But Clinton hoped for something better than that. He was gam-
bling. He hoped that the mutineers would come into the British
army of their own accord if he offered them their back pay in
coin. This offer, on a paper that was enclosed in the lead foil
usually used for wrapping tea, was entrusted to half a dozen
British spies, who made their way to Princeton, while Clinton
waited, cocked, poised, on Staten Island.

Four of the spies actually got into the camp of the mutineers.
Two, supposing, assumedly, that they would be welcomed with

open arms, announced themselves and were taken before the board of sergeants, which ordered them clapped into the guardhouse.

Hearing this, the other two spies in camp dropped their messages and got out.

Joseph Reed, president of the Supreme Executive Council of Pennsylvania, and General James Potter, a member of that council, came from Philadelphia. They were admitted, and joined Wayne and the colonels, whereupon the haggling commenced.

In Philadelphia there was near panic, even after the mutineers had come to a stop at Princeton, where they stayed a whole week, at the end of which time they marched to Trenton, encamping beside the river.

By that time everything had been ironed out. Such men as had truly served three years—and if the enlistment papers had been lost each man's oath would be taken—were to be honorably discharged, with pay. Nobody was punished. It was a complete victory for the mutineers.

As Wayne, who had been arguing with them all the while, told the commander in chief, the mutineers scorned "to turn Arnolds," which, he added, were their own words. Seemingly there never had been a thought of going over to the enemy. The two spies were given to Wayne, who hanged them. And the redcoats and the Hessians, crestfallen, quit Staten Island and went back to Manhattan and to Long Island, their regular quarters. The crisis was past.[13]

There was an aftermath, only a week later, when the three New Jersey regiments of the Continental line quit their barracks at Pompton. They soon returned, but they remained in a state of open rebellion, refusing to obey their officers, demanding back pay, demanding to be released.

They were not as well led, and Washington this time was better prepared. Washington dispatched General Robert Howe to the spot with a force of New Englanders more than twice the size of the three New Jersey regiments, which were surrounded.

Howe's orders were to kill a few mutineers on the spot, as an example. On the advice of their officers he selected one from each regiment, tried them at a drumhead court-martial, right on the parade ground, found them guilty, and ordered them to be shot then and there. This was done in the case of the first two, but the third was pardoned at the last minute.

There was no stirring among the New Jersey men after that.

Chapter Nine

THERE WERE BRAINS on the British side, but they were not well co-ordinated. There were individual talents, some of a high order, but these lacked direction. Personalities played a large part in British military policy, which was bad; and it grew worse as the war lengthened.

Under a king who at best was stubborn, narrow-minded, not to say pig-headed, at the worst was raving mad—a madness as yet kept from the public—the Lord North cabinet was scarcely a felicitous assemblage of intellectual giants; and surely one of its weakest members was Lord George Germain, who under his earlier and better known name of Sackville had been court-martialed for his inaction at the battle of Minden and formally proclaimed to be forever incapable of holding any military office in Great Britain. Soldiers, in consequence, despised Germain. Yet this man presently was secretary of state for the colonies, which meant that he supervised the suppression of the revolt in America, giving orders to admirals and generals who in ordinary life wouldn't have been seen in the same room with him. Germain knew nothing about America—it was a common complaint of the time at Home—and his direction of the war, from three thousand miles away, was erratic, to say the least of it. He was forever changing his mind, and he played favorites shamelessly. Besides, he was not intelligent.

The man in charge of his Majesty's armed forces in America was Sir Henry Clinton, a career soldier, recently knighted, a conscientious, hard-working, if not brilliant general, who had violent likes and dislikes. One of his dislikes was Admiral Marriot Arbuthnot, a fusty, crusty officer who was near seventy and not to be hurried. Clinton simply could not stand the man. In fact, Clinton had written to Lord Germain—whom also he could not abide—that unless Arbuthnot was recalled he, Clinton, must resign. As the year 1780 drew to a close Sir Henry was waiting for his answer. This always took three months or so, often half a year.

(When the answer did come it was in favor of the general, recalling the admiral, who was replaced by Admiral Graves, a man not greatly gifted but who at least had good manners.)

This lack of co-operation between the services, no new thing, was important; but of perhaps even greater importance was the relationship between General Clinton and his second-in-command, Charles Cornwallis, second earl of Cornwallis. These two never would have been close in spirit, but at the beginning, though there was a certain coolness between them, their relations were at least correct. Clinton, the older man, the superior officer, leaned over backward, for a time, in an attempt to assure his titled subordinate that he would not be hampered by a half-dead hand from a distance. Clinton himself when he withdrew into New York in effect stopped fighting, but it was not in the nature of Cornwallis to behave in any such fashion, for Cornwallis, in his mid-forties, was all action. When he left him in conquered Charleston to pursue the war in the south, Clinton adjured Lord Cornwallis never to risk the loss of Charleston itself, but he did not restrict him to the coast, on the contrary giving him permission to range as he thought best. Communications being what they were, this seemed only fair. But Clinton was liberal, even magnanimous. He gave the younger man permission to correspond directly with Lord Germain.

That Clinton kept Cornwallis well supplied with reinforcements was only common sense, for Clinton wasn't really using the men he had, while Cornwallis most certainly was.

When he turned inland, as he did almost as soon as his commander's ship had faded over the northern horizon, one of the reasons Cornwallis gave was that the coast was unhealthy; yet when he cut a wide swath through South Carolina and then even invaded North Carolina, Cornwallis at all times was crippled by a high sick rate, many of his men being carried. The countryside was not at all receptive, as had been expected, and Cornwallis, who liked to travel fast, by that same token liked to travel light, so that his sick not infrequently suffered from lack of medical supplies. He was himself intermittently ill; but he was always energetic.

This was not formal war, not European war laid out on planned, carefully selected battlefields. Rather it was what was known locally as "bush fighting," a series of raids and ambuscades, a rush down from the hills, a disappearance as though by magic into an apparently impenetrable swamp. It was harsh, bitter, a personal war, civil war in short, attended by many harassments, burnings, hangings, even torture. It was feuding on a big scale. Even prisoners were not safe, as when, after the surrender at Kings Mountain, the patriot militia right there on the field hanged nine of the loyalists—not Britishers but neighbors. This shocked Cornwallis, but the militia on either side took it for granted.

These "little wars" were not uncommon in the north. There was a whole series of them, a semipermanent state of warfare, in the Niagara district and in Cherry Valley, New York. The commonwealths of Pennsylvania and Connecticut to all intents and purposes were at war over Wyoming Valley, and there were highly placed persons who favored having New York State secede from the confederation in order that it might spend all its time and energy fighting Ethan Allen and his Green Moun-

tain Boys. Loyalists temporarily living in Staten Island, which
was under British control, thought nothing of crossing the Kill
van Kull into Elizabethtown at night in small parties to rob and
burn and kill. There was an active group of die-hards in a fort
at Bergen Neck, New Jersey, who used to sally forth with some
regularity and lay waste the surrounding, patriot territory.

Each commander in chief, officially at least, frowned upon this
sort of conflict; but it went on. One of the most notorious of the
"little wars" was that waged in Westchester County, New York,
where in a strip of land about thirty miles square, a sort of no
man's land, the Cowboys and the Skinners, partisans, irregular
militiamen, little better than banditti, plundered right and left,
paying off old scores, specializing in livestock, and even sometimes making a pretense of fighting one another. New York
City was crowded with troops and with refugees, and there was
always a demand for food there, a demand the Cowboys, who
had some sort of tenuous connection with the British army,
strove to satisfy with stolen cattle, while the Skinners, who had
an even more tenuous connection with the Continental Army,
strove to steal the cattle back from the Cowboys before it could
be delivered. It was a group of Skinners that had waylaid Major
André when he was trying to get back to the city by land.[14]

However, nowhere were the "little wars" waged with such
ferocity as in Georgia and the Carolinas.

Lord Cornwallis kept moving, and fighting, and he usually
won, though the victories were costly and inconclusive. Moreover, since the recall of Gates he was faced with an opponent
who loved fighting and understood it quite as much as did the
expert earl himself. For Nathanael Greene was proving what
everybody who knew him always had believed—that he had
a flair for this kind of work. His task was discouraging, so far
from base, so badly supplied, with a force that consisted largely
of militiamen who came and went like ghosts, more often, it
would seem, going than coming. But he persisted, building up
his wavering army, and time after time nimbly leaping out of

a trap just before its jaws clanged shut. "We fight, get beaten, and fight again," he reported to Washington.

Cornwallis, it seemed, could not stay still. For weeks on end the worried Clinton, in New York, hardly knew what colony his second-in-command was in, much less what he was doing there. When Clinton in the middle of December dispatched General Alexander Leslie with twenty-five hundred men to Virginia, it was only in part to take the pressure off Cornwallis; it was in part as well to establish a naval base at or near Portsmouth. As Sir Henry now saw it, the best place to pinch the American colonies and crush the rebellion—now that the Hudson was too well fortified—was the narrow "waist" that divided north from south at Maryland. "The Chesapeake," it was generally called in reports and dispatches. That bay, unlike the bay at New York, which was considered to have too high a bar for the really big ships of the line, was deep water everywhere. It would be an ideal jumping-off place for the British, whether north or south. But a base must be built there first. Leslie had been told that he should do this, but he was to be under Cornwallis's control.

Leslie's movements must have puzzled the scouting, troubled Virginians, who did not know whether they should call out the militia, an expensive process. Leslie had landed, foraged a bit, started to survey and even to build, and then suddenly had departed, sailing south. The reason, as they were to learn, was that Cornwallis had sent for him, peremptorily. Yet Cornwallis was the very one who might most need that Chesapeake base, if he should get beyond his depth—if, for example, the French fleet, which had been threatening for three years, actually should come.

Clinton tried again. He sent Benedict Arnold, late in the year, with sixteen hundred men. Arnold met a bad storm and lost almost half of his horses, an important consideration now that the war was shifting south and the leaders at last were beginning to realize the value of cavalry and mounted infantry such as dragoons. He landed, marched up to Richmond, took that town without any resistance, burned right and left, destroyed a cannon foundry, and easily returned to Portsmouth—without a scratch.

This must not be allowed to continue. Something must be done about Arnold, or soon in the south Greene would be cut off and could be torn to pieces by the unremitting Cornwallis.

George Washington went on believing that the war would be settled in New York City, and still hoped to combine with the French at Newport for a large-scale assault on Clinton's garrison; but he could recognize an emergency when he saw one. He decided to authorize a crack corps, a small independent detachment, and put this under the command of a man who had been begging long and loudly for such an assignment—namely, the young Marquis de Lafayette, that "statue walking around in search of a pedestal." To many of his advisers this was like handing a loaded pistol to a baby; but Washington had great faith in and a great fondness for the carrot-headed youngster; so the thing was done.

Lafayette's force would be small, smaller even than the force of Benedict Arnold, but it would be select, whereas Arnold's was largely trash. If he moved fast, and if Arnold was not reinforced by sea, there was just a chance that the marquis might snare the traitor at the end of one of those long narrow peninsulas that characterize tidewater Virginia. It was a small chance, true; but it was provided against in the instructions given to Lafayette February 20, 1881:[15]

> You are to do no act whatever with Arnold that directly or by implication may skreen him from the punishment due to his treason and desertion, which if he should fall into your hands, you will execute in the most summary way.

Just a chance . . .

Chapter Ten

MOST WEST INDIAN islands are beautiful. St. Eustatius is an exception. It consists largely of Quill, a long-extinct volcano with dirty bare white sides. There is no lagoon, there are no beaches, only rubble. Properly speaking there was no harbor or bay of any kind in the eighteenth century, but the Dutch, with their experience with turbulent waters, had built a mole that made the roads a good enough anchorage in all but hurricane weather.

Most Americans in the year 1781, unless they happened to be smugglers, probably could not even pronounce St. Eustatius, much less locate it on a map. Yet when this smudgy marine flyspeck fell to a British fleet, February 3, the shock to the Continental cause was stunning.

St. Eustatius had come to be called the Golden Rock, it was so prosperous. Nobody went there for a vacation, a good time. Men went there either to buy or to sell. The Dutch, who did not know what else to do with St. Eustatius—"Statia" locally—had liberalized it to the point of scandal, and beyond. At St. Eustatius they didn't ask to see your clearance papers, your credentials, only the color of your money. They would outfit almost anybody, and with almost anything, on a no-questions-asked basis. It was what the notorious Port Royal, Jamaica, had been a little earlier, before its earthquake.

Of squirrel guns and fowling pieces and, on the frontier of Pennsylvania, rifles, there were plenty in the American colonies at the start of the Revolution; but there were few rugged, easily reloaded, military muskets, and there was almost no gunpowder at all. It was France that had undertaken to make up these shortages, even in the days before the alliance, though the Dutch themselves often helped. In any case, it was estimated that about half of the enormous supplies of munitions that reached America from Europe were transshipped at St. Eustatius.

Many American privateers, too, got their supplies, as they sold their booty, at St. Eustatius.

Great Britain protested, and the Dutch said that they would look into the matter. Great Britain also protested that many of her own subjects, residents of nearby British colonies, had a clandestine stake in those warehouses on St. Eustatius. The Dutch said that they would look into that, too.

It was at Statia that the Stars and Stripes was first formally recognized by a foreign government. A Yankee brig, *Andrew Doria*, putting in at Oranjestad for reasons of its own, unfurled the brand-new, just-authorized ensign, and the governor, stout Johannes de Graaff, delighted, ordered a salute by the cannons in Fort Oranje.

When word of this reached St. Kitts, a nearby British isle, the governor there protested shrilly. De Graaff brushed this off. The governor of St. Kitts carried his protest all the way to Whitehall, which carried it to Amsterdam through the British ambassador there, Sir Joseph Yorke. The Dutch said that they would look into it. The British persisted, and the Dutch recalled De Graaff for questioning. That examination could hardly have been rigorous. In a little while Johannes de Graaff was back on the Golden Rock, where business was as usual.

To the British, who did not recognize the United States of America and therefore did not recognize the United States navy, Captain John Paul Jones was neither more nor less than a pirate; and when that sensational little officer put in at Amsterdam with two prizes plucked from off the very shores of England, Sir Joseph Yorke went into indignant action once again. The Dutch said that they would look into it. But Jones was there for three months, and was allowed to sell his prizes and to sail away unmolested.

At last the British stopped protesting and declared war on the Netherlands. That was December 20, 1780, and a fast dispatch boat was immediately sent off to the West Indies to inform Admiral Rodney and to instruct him to grab everything Dutch in sight, starting—the instructions were specific here—with St. Eustatius.

Rodney at the head of an overwhelming fleet arrived off Oranjestad February 3. It was a complete surprise, nobody there having heard about the war, and the fort struck. There were almost a hundred and fifty vessels in port, and all of these were of course seized, while several warships were sent after a convoy of about thirty vessels that had sailed two days before—and they overtook this and brought it back.

Oranjestad was one street about a mile long, lined on both sides by stone warehouses. Not only were all of those warehouses crammed with confiscatable goods to the last cubic inch of space, but some of the less perishable goods actually were stored out in the street itself. The haul was tremendous. Rodney estimated it at well over three million pounds. Moreover, he and the British military leader, Vaughan, elected to keep the Dutch flag flying from Fort Oranje for two months after taking the town, so that scarcely a day passed but what some innocent vessel, whose master had not heard that the Netherlands was at war, came stumbling into the roadstead—and capture.

Because so many of the goods seized proved to be the property of British subjects, Rodney was to be plastered with lawsuits for a long while to come, and there were some tart questions asked in the House of Commons; but none of this did any good to the poor Yankee privateers who had thus so suddenly lost their favorite base.

Negligently, languidly, without even looking up from the main prize, Rodney also seized the two nearby Dutch islands of Saba and St. Martin.

There was yet another way in which the taking of St. Eustatius was to have a powerful effect upon the destiny of the American people. Sir George Rodney was an inveterate and unlucky gambler and his financial affairs were in a deplorable state, yet even at the best of times he was hardly averse to lining his pockets by anything less than out-and-out piracy: he had caused his son to be appointed a naval staff-captain, with all the emoluments that exalted position brought, the son being aged fifteen. St. Eustatius, then, with its loose wealth, fascinated him. He *said* that the reason he lingered so long on the Golden Rock was because he deemed it advisable to destroy the mole and dismantle the warehouses, which otherwise, retaken by the enemy, might be used again for the same nefarious purposes; but nobody took this seriously. At any rate, when he learned in April that De Grasse at last had broken out of Brest and was making for the West Indies he did nothing to strengthen his second-in-command, Sir Samuel Hood, who was on blockade duty off Fort Royal, the capital of Martinique, the logical destination for De Grasse. True, neither Hood nor Rodney knew that the French admiral had so large a fleet—twenty ships of the line— but it is true too that if Rodney had not been listening so closely to the jingling of the guinea at Statia he would have been with Hood, who, as it happened, greatly outnumbered, had to let the French fleet escape unscathed. Had the other warships been there, together with the admiral—for Rodney, if he was weak at strategy, was a master tactician—the result would have been quite different. Rodney would either have destroyed the French fleet or so badly mauled it that it would have had to return home for a refitting[16] and so abandon its purposed relief trip to the Virginia capes. But Rodney was counting coins; and De Grasse got through.

Chapter Eleven

THE CUSTOM WAS to divide an infantry regiment into regulars and light infantry, the latter to be perhaps a fifth or a sixth of the whole. The light infantry were not necessarily *physically* light, but they were fast-moving, the van, the scouts, those who were selected for special work—in effect, an elite corps. They

wore no special uniform or insignia, though sometimes they
were paid (or promised) more money than the regulars.

In the British army, as in the various mercenary German
groups,[17] the two end companies of a regiment drawn up in
parade formation were known as the light infantry and the
grenadiers. The grenadiers no longer carried grenades. Far
from being lighter than the average, they were picked in part
for their great size; their tallness was calculated to scare the
enemy and hence was exaggerated by the special steeple hats
they wore. They, however, were used for the same purposes as
the light infantry, with whom they often worked. They were
special service troops. For example, that memorable force sent
out of Boston the night of April 18-19, 1775, to destroy the
rebels' concentration of supplies at Concord, was made up
entirely of light infantry and grenadier companies.

The men who assembled February 19, 1781, at Peekskill,
were light infantry, some six hundred of them, all from New
England.

They crossed the river next day, making for Ramapo.

Such a movement of men—a large one as this war went—
could not fail to attract the attention of British spies, who were
everywhere. However, the secret was well kept. The men were
not given any instructions except marching orders at the last
minute, and they were not issued any special equipment. Most
of them supposed that they were destined to make another try
at conquering Staten Island, the previous one, a month before,
having failed because of lack of boats. That Lafayette was to be
their commanding officer strengthened this belief among the
men and the officers, as well, probably, as at British headquarters; for Lafayette had headed the abortive raid—a raid
that never really got started—and he had been furious at this
failure, no fault of his own, so that it seemed only natural to
give him another chance. Even the colonels did not know the
truth.

On the twenty-third they reached Pompton, New Jersey, and
there they were joined by about two hundred light infantry-

men of the New Jersey line. There was hard feeling right away between the Pompton men and those from the other side of the Hudson. This was usual. Their neighbors, the New Jerseyites and New Yorkers, hated all New Englanders with a hatred much more virulent than ever the Southerners displayed.

Lafayette himself joined them and addressed them at Pompton, and the group was broken into three battalions. Standards were passed out. Lafayette's men always were better clothed than the generality of Continental soldiers, because he paid for a good part of it out of his own pocket.

The next stop was Hanover, New Jersey, and then Morristown, where they rested a little.

By this time the men had begun to realize that they were going to some place farther away than Staten Island. Most of them were elated by this thought, though there was some grumbling that they had not been given time to prepare for a long trip: the officers, in particular, were woefully short of cash.

Then Somerville, where they were joined by another contingent of the New Jersey line, and so to Princeton, where the feeling between the two factions erupted in a riot. Lafayette was not there, having gone ahead to Philadelphia to arrange for artillery and supplies, but the officers, after a couple of wild hours, managed to get the men in hand.

Except for this unpleasantness, which was without fatalities, they marched well, like the veterans they in fact were. All the way to Trenton, where they were to take another rest, there were no sick and only two stragglers, who soon rejoined the army.

The artillery "park" taken on at Philadelphia was made up of twelve heavy and six small cannons and the men to move and to man them. Why these were taken, what use they would be in the pursuit of so elusive an officer as Benedict Arnold in so low and wet a country as tidewater Virginia, nobody tried to explain. It was customary to have cannons, that's all. Though there were no sieges and the distances were so great in this land of many hills and streams and forests and swamps, the tremendous labor of moving those massive pieces from place to place, from Boston and Dorchester all the way down to Savannah, not to mention the balls and the vast quantities of precious gunpowder they ate, were taken for granted.

The influence of the redoubtable Brigadier Henry Knox, chief of artillery, no doubt had something to do with this unrealistic attitude; but even more telling must have been the conventional view of war, of warfare, which assumed artillery, no matter what the conditions. You were not a real army, you were simply a pack of armed peasants—so the reasoning ran— if you did not have cannons.

These pieces and the large force of men that was required to handle them, a force that brought the total of this legion up to twelve hundred, were sent ahead, by water much of the way, to Head of Elk, Maryland,[18] the northernmost point of Chesapeake Bay. The infantry, which could move so much faster by itself, rested a bit at Trenton.

There was another reinforcement that had been expected at Philadelphia, several hundred men of the Pennsylvania line, but these were not forthcoming. The reason was the recent mutiny, which had resulted in virtually every rank-and-filer of the Pennsylvania line being mustered out, since even those who actually had enlisted for the duration swore that it had been only for three years—and according to the terms of the agreement reached at Princeton a man's oath was all that was needed. These men would re-enlist, many of them, perhaps most of them, Major General Arthur St. Clair, their commanding officer, told Lafayette. They should be ready soon, after they had visited with the folks back home and had spent their money. St. Clair's second-in-command, Anthony Wayne, who would lead these troops to Virginia, even promised a thousand of them; but then, Wayne always had been a big talker.

The infantry dropped down the river in barges, from Trenton to Wilmington, Delaware, from where they marched, in an icy rain, to Head of Elk.

Here Lafayette was met by a whole cloud of delays, the chief of which was an utter lack of boats. He never hesitated. Indeed, this ebullient young man was doing a wonderful job of all the tiresome and vexatious details connected with moving an army overland. The men were beginning to believe in him, which had not always been the case. His English improved in great linguistical leaps and bounds, so that his accent had become only quaint. The civilian population, and especially the merchants, the ones he had chiefly to deal with now, adored him. He was anything but prepossessing, but his youth, his prestige as an aristocrat, a rich one to boot, and most of all his passionate earnestness, caused all sorts of persons to pitch in and help him. Nor did his open admiration for the soldiers of the Continental army—"they have a patience in their misery which is unknown in European armies," he wrote to Vergennes—do him any harm.

Even here, as he was assembling a "navy" and persuading a temporarily unattached commodore to command it, as he was dickering with Baltimore businessmen and bowing before and saying flattering things to their wives, talking them into making shirts for his men—even here he was threatened with yet another resounding failure, he who was so agonized in his search for fame. His instructions were to try to grab Arnold—but only if the French fleet out of Newport, or some not inconsiderable part of it, should previously have cut off Arnold's retreat by sea. If the French did not appear off the Virginia capes, then Lafayette was to return, with his whole force, to be ready to join the hoped-for attack on New York.

He was ahead of schedule, that's true. The men had marched so well, the civilians had co-operated so handsomely, that he was at Head of Elk long before Washington—or Destouches, the French naval commander—could have expected. All the same, the news from Virginia, where Steuben with five thousand militiamen had Arnold bottled up at Portsmouth, was disconcerting. Not only had no French ships been sighted but there were even a few English ones out there. Moreover, Steuben, who could have done with a little glory himself, since he was a professional, international soldier, was talking of storming Arnold's

lines and nabbing the traitor on his own. Lafayette would
supersede Steuben in the supreme command when he reached
Virginia, but would he reach Virginia in time? What was to
prevent Steuben from jumping the gun and making himself
immortal? The marquis had some unhappy moments, there at
Head of Elk.

However, the fleet was assembled and the happy word was
received—from Washington direct—that the French actually
had sailed.

With a whoop he was on his way.

He hastened ahead, a trick of his, with a few aides and a mere
handful of soldiers. This was his "army" when after various
misadventures he at last approached the Yorktown peninsula
in an open boat. There he was almost drowned, at the last
moment. In his eagerness to get ashore first he started to swim
his horse to land, but the beast shied and threw him.[19] The
Marquis de Lafayette couldn't swim a stroke. Fortunately some
of the soldiers who could fished him out.

Wet then, though his ardor was undampened, he scrambled
up the beach. He spread his feet, and fisted his hips. He looked
around.

Well, where was this Benedict Arnold?

Chapter Twelve

MANY A MAN, AT the beginning, had urged upon George Washington the idea of a mountain war, bush fighting. The colonies,
it was argued, never could hope to beat the British at their
own game of heavy-equipment, massed warfare. Anyway, the
country, with its hills and swamps, its streams and forests, and
its appalling roads, was not fitted for this. Washington did not
agree. To his neat mind, to his fastidious if provincial taste, .

there was something vulgar about such tactics. They were not
for gentlemen. Moreover, he was determined to prove to the
rest of the world that Americans could be as formal in their
fighting as anybody else, and were not, truly, a pack of blood-
thirsty, howling takers of scalps.[20] Also, Washington liked the
pageantry of army life. He was quite willing and even eager
to use hit-and-run tactics in the field itself, and to encourage
ambuscades and night marches. He was especially fond of sur-
prises, which sometimes were successful, as at Trenton, and
sometimes, as at Germantown, not. But for shrieking, the
brandishment of tomahawks, he had no use.

It is the more remarkable, then, that he had remained, almost
to the end, unaware of the value of cavalry, an arm that, after
all, used more pageantry than any other. Washington was himself a superb horseman, and he came from a horse-loving colony,
for it was to Virginia that the first thoroughbreds were im-
ported, and it was in Virginia—and in neighboring Maryland
—that the first horse races in this land were held, the first fox
hunts organized. True, when Washington took over the command it was at the siege of Boston, one of the two times—the
very beginning of the war and the very end—when artillery
was important while cavalry was not. It was true too that his
first experience with mounted volunteers was unfortunate, for
these were likely to be fancy small outfits of fops from the cities,
lads who were more interested in their plumes and sashes than
in their duties as scouts. Again, perhaps Washington—he was so
reserved a man that nobody could be sure—was in agreement
with many of his best military advisers, who believed that the
war would be fought largely in the north, Maine, Vermont, the
Adirondacks, which was hardly the best terrain for horses, or,
if the British won at first, in the mountains of western Pennsylvania, another district scarcely suited to cavalry. All the same,
he could have used many a mounted unit in his campaigns in
New Jersey and around New York, for his Intelligence was never
of the best.

When the war moved south this was changed. There the

countryside was more open, the fields more flat, and the distances even greater than in the north. The war in the Carolinas,
not altogether unexpectedly, gave birth to some gifted maneu-
verers who relied upon the horse.

A distinction must be made, and maintained, between cavalry
and mounted infantry.

Almost no cavalry was used in the War of the American
Revolution.

In the first place, there were not many horses, and most of the
horses there were, were draft horses, not saddle horses. This was
the case even in Maryland and Virginia. A cavalryman fought
on his horse, *with* his horse. That is to say, both man and animal
struggled. They had to be trained for this, separately and together; and the horse, which might frequently have more sense
than its rider, could not see any reason for the training, and
that made it long and expensive.

Even if many horses could be trained for conflict, what
weapons would be used? Pistols were costly, and they were tricky
toys that could not be counted upon. The lance and the saber
were all very well for the parklike regions of Europe, but they
would hardly do in rugged America, even in the south. Rifles
and muskets were unthinkable. Even the Tower musket of the
British army, the Brown Bess, with its 39-inch barrel, measured
almost 60 inches from butt to muzzle, and this was esteemed a
prodigy of compactness: the American muskets and rifles (there
were not many rifles on either side) were not standardized, but
the shortest of them was much longer than the Brown Bess, and
much heavier.

Mounted infantry, or dragoons, were different. Unless they
were surprised, they fought on foot. It was a matter of trans-
portation. Even a plow horse can go faster and farther, and carry
more weight, than a pedestrian. And those plow horses could
be tethered and tended by pre-appointed hostlers while the
dragoons themselves advanced into battle with their muskets,
using the same tactics as any other infantrymen.

What was more, the dragoon not only could get there faster, he

could leave faster as well. If the troops all around him panicked
—and this might happen in the best of regulated armies—the
dragoon knew that he was not likely to be bayoneted right then
and there on the field by a wild, oncoming, victory-drunk
enemy, for he had his mount. After some disastrous defeat,
such as Gates suffered at Camden, the mounted infantry almost
always got away intact. It was one reason why men liked that
service, and sought it. "You live longer," they would say.

The British in the course of their romp through Virginia and
the Carolinas took the trouble to impress every horse they could
get their hands on. Two of the most active of their officers,
each a lieutenant colonel, controlled forces that were largely
mounted: John Graves Simcoe with his Queen's Rangers, all
loyalists, in green uniforms turned over with blue, and tall
leather caps, had come south with Arnold, while the dark,
fierce, disagreeable Banastre Tarleton was with Cornwallis.
Through posts and villages and past crossroads with curious
names—Ninety-Six, Hanging Rock (at this skirmish there was
present on the patriot side a thirteen-year-old boy named
Andrew Jackson, who found that he liked strife so much that
he was never to desist from it), Bird's Ordinary, Eutaw Springs,
Point of Fork, Albermarle Old Court House—these men can-
tered or galloped, moving great distances at a speed no foot
soldiers could have matched.

Cornwallis had gone as far north as Charlotte, on the road to
Salisbury, when news of Kings Mountain caused him at last to
draw rein. He even retreated a little, back into South Carolina
as far as Winnsboro, and there allowed his men a little rest.

In sober truth, and though his movements had been sensational, he was in an uncomfortable position just then. He had
to keep more than a dozen posts garrisoned, some of them
strongly, which left his actual, tactical striking force a small one,
though it was extremely efficient, and at its lowest it remained
larger than the regular force opposed to it. Again and again he
had issued a call for all local royalists to come in and prove
their loyalty by taking up a musket, and again and again he had

got next to nobody. The sickness in his ranks increased, with another summer looming. His own health was none too good. He was very far from any real base, and far from the sea. Worst of all, he found himself fencing with an enemy who was most marvelously adroit and who seemed to guess each move Cornwallis made even before he made it.

The slow-grinning Greene, the Quaker from Rhode Island, was slow about nothing else. He too put great faith in mounted troops, and he too was served by a couple of spirited, imaginative, and exceedingly active equestrians. These were both Virginians, both colonels, Henry ("Light-Horse Harry") Lee[21] and William Washington, a rich planter, a relative of the commander in chief. William Washington's force, a small one, fewer than 150 men most of the time, was true cavalry—and all dash. Repeatedly, thrown into the fray at the last minute, it was to prove a tide-turner. It was that way, for example, at Cowpens, January 17, another field that gave the noble earl pause.

Greene could be counted upon to do the unexpected, but when he cut his small force into two separate armies and sent them in different directions, it looked as though he had ventured upon the suicidal. He had only about fifteen hundred men altogether, when first he took command in the south, but he had guerrilla militiamen who were familiar with the land and who could make themselves as ephemeral as fireflies—Pickens, Sumter, Marion. He had also yet another Virginian (though this one had been born in New Jersey), the tough, iron-jawed Daniel Morgan. No cavalryman, Morgan nonetheless was not a soldier to waste time. Commissioned early in the war, he had marched his men from Williamsburg to Boston in twenty-one days. Later, in command of a brigade, he marched this all the way from Saratoga, New York, to the Continental camp at Whitemarsh, Pennsylvania, in eighteen days, an average of twelve miles a day—and that in late fall and with full equipment.

Disgusted with Congress, Colonel Morgan recently had thrown up his commission, but private life had proved too tame for him and when Gates was in trouble in South Carolina, Morgan volunteered to help. He was now Nathanael Greene's right-hand man. It was Morgan whom Greene appointed to the command of the other half of his bisected army.

Cornwallis, scarcely believing in his own good luck, decided to stamp out that half first, Morgan's half. He sent after it the feared Tarleton.

Tarleton, like his chief, was a driver; and perhaps on this occasion he drove his men too hard. Like Cornwallis again, he expected wonders—which they often got—of the British soldier. But Tarleton's men were tired when at last they caught up with Morgan at a place called Cowpens. And Morgan for his part was tired of running away from them. He turned.

He had planned the thing well. His numbers were almost equal, now, to those of the British. There was a river at his back, the Broad River, making retreat difficult if not impossible; but he had meant to have it that way, for he thought that the men would fight better if they were desperate.

He had no outposts to pull in. His first line, a double one, was made up of militiamen from Georgia and the Carolinas, raw troops in whom he had little confidence. He told them that they must fire at least twice, and he posted riflemen behind them to shoot any who started to run away before that—a common practice of the time. As a matter of fact, they did more than Morgan had asked of them, firing many volleys before they fell back in good order through prepared holes in the second line. They were under the command of Brigadier General Andrew Pickens.

The second line was made up of veteran Virginia militiamen and Continental regulars from farther north, Maryland and Delaware. Facing down a slight slope, they never wavered. Their fire was terrific. Yet doggedly, with heavy losses, the British came on.

Because of a misunderstanding of commands the patriots, who were shifting their positions, appeared to be in retreat at last.

With shouts of triumph, their bayonets gleaming, the deluded British charged.

They came too fast. They broke ranks in their excitement. And the Americans mowed them down in swaths.

The redcoats broke. Raging among them, Tarleton tried to get them to charge once more—just once more.

At that moment William Washintgon, who had been screened behind a small hill with his 125 cavalrymen, rode gloriously into the fray in his traditional role of balance-tipper. And at the same time the original first line, the Carolina and Georgia boys under Pickens, who meanwhile had marched clear across the American rear, suddenly appeared on Tarleton's right and began to blaze away, getting back into a fight they had never really wished to leave.

The British broke and ran. It was a rout. Tarleton's losses were some nine hundred, besides all his equipment, including a couple of field guns. The patriot losses were no more than a handful. As usual, only the mounted men escaped. And Daniel Morgan was able to report, accurately enough if gloatingly, that he had given the British "a devil of a whipping."

Chapter Thirteen

BENEDICT ARNOLD'S rather contemptible force—Arnold, who had been offered the whole left wing of the Continental army! —was cooped in Portsmouth, and it was short of provisions. It could not last long, by itself. A break-out seemed to be unthinkable, though the wary Steuben had taken every precaution again surprise, continually strengthening his works.

The traitor himself might have been reconciled to surrender —and death.

"What would your men do with me, if they should catch me?" he asked a prisoner, a Continental captain.

The reply was unpleasant.

"We would cut off the leg that you had hurt in the service of your country, and we'd hang the rest of you."

There were reports, recently verified, that Arnold was about to be reinforced by about three thousand regulars under Major General William Phillips, and that these reinforcements were already being assembled in New York. But Phillips could not land, and Arnold and his men necessarily would fall without any loss, once the French fleet had taken up a position off the capes. Where *was* that fleet, by the way?

Just at first Lafayette was faced with a thick, prickly Baron Friedrich Wilhelm Ludolf Gerhard Augustin von Steuben, who, though he was not well liked by the Virginians, who winced at his accent, his barbarous bluntness, nevertheless had done an excellent task of raising the Virginia militia, an exceptionally touchy body, and using it to corner Arnold. True, the militiamen's terms of service would soon run out, when no doubt they would all go home, but Lafayette's force of regulars, now, would be enough to take care of the trapped traitor.

Catch Arnold! Catch the villain!

It was a situation that called for tact at headquarters. Steuben was more than twice Lafayette's age and had been a full-time professional soldier all his life, the veteran of half a hundred battles, whereas Lafayette never had heard a shot fired in anger until he came to America, and the highest military rank he had held at that time was captain of reserves. Steuben's title of baron was false, as much a part of his professionalism as were his epaulets; Lafayette's title of marquis was real. The one was penniless, the other very rich. Each was a major general in the Continental army, but the Frenchman's commission predated that of the German, which meant that Lafayette would automatically take command.

This, just at first, Lafayette refused to do. He pointed out, with impeccable grace, that Baron von Steuben was so familiar

with the local situation that it would be no more than good
sense for him to continue in charge—at least for a while. He
praised Steuben's dispositions, and wrote to Washington suggesting that *he* praise them, which Washington promptly proceeded to do. Thus equanimity was maintained.

Thorny too, though more interesting as more complex, was
the governor of Virginia, a long, gangling, sandy-faced man who
was reluctant to extend the privilege of military impressment
from ten miles to twenty-five—though the British of course
simply took whatever they could lay their hands on—and who
did not believe, anyway, that many more supplies would be
forthcoming from the Old Dominion, whose militiamen, too,
he doubted would stay on. This man, Thomas Jefferson by
name, as a framer of public statements was unexcelled, but he
did not make a good wartime executive—at least, from
Lafayette's point of view.

At last the warships appeared, eight of them, and dropped
anchor in Lynnhaven Bay, just inside of Cape Henry. But—
and the blow must have staggered many more than the easily
staggered Marquis de Lafayette—they were not French, they
were English. Arbuthnot at last had been stirred into action.
And—where was Destouches?

These vessels had been in a fight, scouts reported. Almost
every one of them had been hulled, and some were barely afloat,
while their tars were feverishly working to repair their rigging,
shot to ribbons. This had happened recently, just a little while
ago, the scouts said. There were no shore parties.

The following day, though some of them limped, these
vessels sailed out of Lynnhaven Bay and made for the open sea,
where they were lost to sight. Soon afterward a distant can-
nonading was heard, and it lasted for three hours. Obviously,
then, the French were out there, and the battle had been joined.
Those at Yorktown waited with held breath. Which ships would
come in?

A great many came, far more than had gone away, but the
warships among them were English. The others were transports,

the reinforcements under General Phillips. It was to greet this
convoy that the crippled warships had left Lynnhaven Bay.

There had indeed been a fight at sea, outside the capes, but
it had been earlier, and the sounds the anxious patriots heard
were only thunder.

The fight took place March 16, when the British fleet of eight
ships of the line, under Arbuthnot, sighted a French fleet of the
same size behind them and a bit farther out to sea, making, as
the English were, for the entrance to Chesapeake Bay, the space
of about twenty miles between Cape Henry on the south, Cape
Charles on the north. The English fleet instantly wheeled about
and made for the French, aggression being with them a tradition. The French drew out in line of battle.

There was then a great deal of jockeying for position, a
process that took almost all day. The seas were running high,
and visibility was poor. The wind at first had been from the
south or the southwest, giving the British the weather gauge,
but before any shots were fired it shifted to the *north*west, giving the *French* the weather gauge. This the French, after wearing, deliberately threw away, relining to the leeward of the
British. Destouches's purpose must have been patent at the
time, yet nobody did anything to block the move.

They knew one another well. There were no secrets. Both
in size of ships and in guns the British were superior. Moreover,
all eight of their vessels were copper-sheathed—only two of
the French ships were—and so could move faster; and perhaps
too they were better handled. Inexplicably—it was later to be
put down as a misundersetanding of signals—the British did
not get in close. It was too choppy for boarding; but the British
advantage in guns was chiefly in carronades rather than long
guns, and carronades were only good at close quarters. Destouches's shift to leeward had made the need for a close fight
even more obvious. In that position, the vessels all being heeled
over at about thirty degrees, the Frenchman could open his
lower gun ports, where the biggest guns were, something that

the Englishman could not do. Nevertheless, the British stayed away, the fools.

It was a confused and confusing fight, and there was nothing decisive, though on the whole the French had the better of it. Yet the British fleet, whether by design or by luck, succeeded in its mission, whereas the French fleet failed. When night came the British were near the capes, the French farther out, and the French wheeled and went north, the direction of Newport. They meant to refit. The British, more seriously mauled, but still game, lumbered into Chesapeake Bay.

Now there was nothing that could prevent the landing of Phillips' troops, seasoned men.

Lafayette's heart was broken. With Steuben's militiamen about to go home in large numbers, he would not be able to operate at all against Phillips, only retreat, while Benedict Arnold suddenly seemed as far away as the man on the moon. If Wayne came, with the promised Pennsylvanians— But even then Lafayette would be heavily outnumbered.

Steuben spoke up. Why not march south, to help Greene in North Carolina for a little while, in this way at least making use of the last days of the militia? The militia were no longer any good *here,* were they? And Phillips and his just-landed troops would hardly be able to follow them very closely, for a while.

Lafayette thought it was a fine idea.

The Virginia council did not agree. The Virginia council could not see sending guns and militiamen out of the state when a formidable British force had just started an invasion. The "no" was flat, without qualification.

The Marquis de Lafayette sighed, and prepared to start back to New York.

Chapter Fourteen

IN WARFARE THERE are many vital places on the enemy at which to shoot, but perhaps the most vulnerable of these is the pocketbook. America had no gold or silver mines, no obvious, convenient source of wealth. Services, shipbuilding, agriculture: these are what had kept the country alive and even caused it to expand, but they were assets of which there had been no reserve and they were easily choked off by the might of the British navy. Yet it costs money to run a war. Patriotic fervor will go just so far; and after that, cash is called for.

One of the first and pleasantest ways to raise funds was by the confiscation of Tory property. This was done on a large scale throughout all thirteen of the colonies. There were a large number of out-and-out or strongly suspected loyalists scattered everywhere. There could be no firm figure, but it was in general assumed that at the beginning of hostilities one third of the inhabitants of the colonies were for independence, one third were against it, and the remaining third was indifferent. The patriots, the independence men, were better organized, more zealous, and conceivably less scrupulous. It has been estimated that more than one hundred thousand Tories were either killed or forced to flee the country—an ejection comparable in its sweep to that of the Acadians from Nova Scotia, the Huguenots from France, even the Moors from Spain in 1492. Many of these were rich. Yet they ran out, after a while, as did their lands, their cattle, and houses. Without this source of funds, the patriots had to resort to the printing press.

France was a mountain of help. The year of the French alliance, Congress cut its military expenditure to less than one-third of what it had previously been; and while Nathanael Greene was hayrick-hopping all over the Carolinas, and the Marquis de Lafayette was venturing into Virginia, that land of lovely names—the Pamunkey, Goose Creek, the Fluvanna, the Mattaponi, the Chickahominy, Ground Squirrel Bridge, Three-

Notched Road, Raccoon Ford, the Rappahannock, Thorough-
fare Gap—France was in fact spending on the American Revolution each year at least four times as much as all thirteen of
the colonies put together were spending.[22] But France was in a
tight fiscal spot herself. She couldn't keep up such expenditure.
She didn't have it.

When he slashed his disdainful way from Portsmouth to
Richmond and back, Benedict Arnold had made it a point never
to miss a tobacco warehouse. They burned well, a fragrant fire.
But this was not wanton! It was legitimate warfare. Tobacco,
still confined for practical purposes to Virginia, was one of the
few reliable sources of wealth. It would keep for a long while
in a storehouse, and in that form it in effect *was* money. By
destroying it Arnold was helping to destroy the American will
to fight.

In the Carolinas it was different. The crops there were either
too skimpy or too bulky to be carried away, and there would
be no sense in burning what was left of them anyway, for the
"little wars" men had burned virtually everything already and
there was no place to apply the busy British torch. In the Carolinas the invader concentrated upon another obvious, point-at-
able, countable source of wealth—Negro slaves. These were
rounded up in large numbers and "liberated" by being sent,
for the most part, to West Indian plantations. That this often
was done in a holier-than-thou, holding-the-nose manner did
not make it any the less valid as a method of waging war.

The farther he got from the sea, from his bases at Wilmington and Charleston, the more difficult it became for Cornwallis
to handle this living booty, which raiders in many cases sought
to snatch back. Nevertheless, he pressed on.

The battle of Cowpens, like that of Kings Mountain, in
neither of which he had participated personally, was a blow to
Lord Cornwallis. This time, however, he did not fall back, as he
had done before; instead he went after Daniel Morgan himself.

Morgan, pushed, thought of taking to the mountains—he
never considered surrender, of course—but Greene had antici-

pated this move on the part of Cornwallis and quickly rejoined his subordinate with some reinforcements under General Huger. Even then, the combined forces were not strong enough to face Cornwallis, as Greene was sorely tempted to do, so they went on retreating, nimbly dodging just out of reach at the last minute. It was almost as though Greene, that unrepentant Quaker, was thumbing his nose at the earl. Yet he had a high respect for Cornwallis! "A modern Hannibal," he called him in a letter to Lafayette.

The modern Hannibal was behaving that way, like a generalissimo. He never asked advice, never requested permission to do anything, and his letters to his superior, far away in New York, were increasingly curt. Cornwallis had sent an aide, a Captain Alexander Ross, to London with official news of the battle of Camden—that resounding British victory, and now the aide was back—the battle had been fought August 16 and Captain Ross rejoined his boss December 21, a prodigy of speed—with news that the Cornwallis stock was extremely high in parliamentary and cabinet circles, the Clinton stock correspondingly low. From that time on Lord Cornwallis became lordly indeed.[23]

Greene on his retreat to the north had paused at Guilford Courthouse, near the place where Ready Creek and Troublesome Creek fall together to make the Haw. He had paced the ground there, thinking what a fine place it would be for a battle. But he had decided against this. He was still too weak. He went north, gathering militia to him, and in another of those masterworks of evasion crossed the Dan just ahead of Cornwallis's advance guard. Greene was now in Virginia, though far from Lafayette, Steuben, Muhlenberg. There at last he was reinforced.

Cornwallis, too far out, could only fall back, south again. This he did, though it was not the sort of campaign he would have preferred.

Greene went after him, snapping.

Greene came again to that field he had liked so well, near the

Guilford Courthouse, and there he spread his men in a formation of defense, facing south. He was ready, at last, to stand and slug it out.

Cornwallis asked nothing better. He turned immediately and by forced marches hurried north, and he attacked the patriots on the morning of March 15.

The patriots outnumbered his forces by more than two to one, but Cornwallis's men were tough, experienced redcoats and Hessians, whereas almost two-thirds of the Americans were raw militia.

Greene, who had Morgan at his side, placed his men much as Morgan had done at Cowpens, though Greene, fortunately, left an avenue of retreat. There was the first thin line of militia, backed by riflemen with orders to shoot into them in the event of an early scare and, again as at Cowpens, they were ordered to fire at least twice before they fell back to prepared positions. This they did. The second line performed even better than had been expected, counterattacking several times with the bayonet; but these men too at last retired, in good order. The third line, upon which Greene counted, held for a long while.

It was a British day, technically. It would go down in history as a British win. Yet the patriots never did panic, though in time they were driven from the field. In fact, the British had gained nothing, no objective, and could not even stay where they were afterward. They had *proved* nothing, except that they were stout fighters, which all the world knew anyway. And one more such "victory" would have ruined them, for their losses had been terrible, their casualties almost thirty per cent, including some of Cornwallis's most valuable officers. They did not pursue Greene. They had no inclination, either, to stand there and huzza. They retreated to the sea they never should have left, making Wilmington in easy stages.

And so things were just about where they had been when Nathanael Greene went south, four months before.

Cornwallis rested only a little while. The logical thing for him to do now, the textbook thing, was to proceed south and west to visit and perhaps occasionally strengthen the sundry British forts and strong points established across South Carolina—Camden, Charleston, Ninety-Six, Orangeburg, Fort Granby, Fort Watson, Fort Georgetown—for these points were scattered and clearly Greene would strive to snap them up one by one in the absence of a covering army. Protecting such points would not have been exciting, but it would have been sensible. It would gain no glory, but at least it would in a businesslike manner see to the retention of gains already made.

Cornwallis thought it over. He had never been timid. He had invaded North Carolina three times, without notable results. He believed that he could never take that colony, the way he had taken South Carolina, so long as North Carolina was being supplied from the north, from Virginia. He believed most fervently that the Chesapeake region, the "waist," was what should be pinched, even at the cost of evacuating New York. He had heard of the landing of Phillips with reinforcements for Arnold.

He decided to go to Virginia. He wrote to Phillips to meet him at Petersburg. Then, early in April, he started north.

It was the greatest military mistake of the war.

Chapter Fifteen

LAFAYETTE HAD LEFT his men at Annapolis, and now he rejoined them, eager to get back to New York, for like Washington he believed that that great occupied city would be the next and possibly final point of attack—and hence of honor—especially so since he had heard from friends in France that the second French division was on its way to America.

He went by way of Mount Vernon, for he wished to meet the relatives of his hero, "and above all your mother," and he made up the time by riding half a night.

It was April 3 when he reached Annapolis, but for one reason or another it was the eighth before he had managed to get his force back to Head of Elk, where another letter from Washington met him, a letter that changed everything. Lafayette was being ordered south again.

It was not like George Washington to reverse orders so abruptly. He was a deliberate and a stubborn man. Here he had at least three reasons.

The attack on New York City looked farther away than ever.

There was a certain amount of jealousy over young Lafayette at the Continental headquarters, especially on the part of Major General William Heath, who outranked the Frenchman and who would gladly have had that independent command himself. Perhaps it was as well to keep the marquis away a little longer.

Probably the most telling reason was Nathanael Greene, who had written begging for reinforcements which could not of course be sent by sea. Lafayette was halfway there; let him go on. But the commander in chief added that Lafayette might operate independently in Virginia, as originally planned, provided General Greene gave his consent. Washington, like Greene, had heard of the landing of Phillips, and like Greene he feared that the Quaker might be crushed between two forces. Lafayette could serve as a diversion. Washington of course did not know at this time that Cornwallis had so suddenly decided to march into Virginia. He could hardly be expected to guess such a move. Nor could anybody else, least of all Lieutenant General Sir Henry Clinton.

There was also a letter direct from Greene, who *did* consent to let Lafayette operate independently in Virginia—at least for the present.

Lafayette was delighted. His men were not. They had left Westchester County, New York, with the understanding that they would be gone only a few days. Despite their commander's most beguiling endeavors, and a liberal use of his own funds, their clothes were in pitiful condition; and they had not been paid in many months. The news that they were going home, or approximately home, had made them very happy. They had actually started north. And now—

They didn't like it. They dreaded the notorious summers of the South which, it was widely reported, could kill a man. They had done nothing, and they wanted to go back. There was a rash of desertions.

The weather also interfered, rains making a morass of the roads and so swelling the Susquehanna that for several days the ferry did not operate. "I have crossed the Rubicon!" Lafayette cried when at last he did get over. He had always been fond of classical allusions.

Phillips and Arnold, no longer obliged to cower on a low peninsula, were raiding and burning right and left as they advanced up the valley of the James, specializing, as Arnold had before, in tobacco warehouses. Clearly their objective was Richmond, which was virtually undefended. Lafayette left his heavy equipment behind, impressed all the wagons he could get, and pushed his men as much as twenty-eight miles a day in his effort to get to Richmond first. There weren't enough wagons or horses. Half the men would ride half the time, while the others walked, and then they would change.

Lafayette was shocked when he learned that Mount Vernon had been spared the torch only because Lund Washington, the commander in chief's nephew and caretaker, had bought the British off with provisions, so that the only things missing were a few slaves who had run away. Lafayette wrote to General Washington about this, but Washington, who had heard, already had reproved his nephew.

Aside from his hatred of all Englishmen, the Marquis de Lafayette had a special reason for hating General Phillips, an old, unrelenting man, a martinet. The marquis's father had been killed at Minden—torn to pieces by an English cannon ball. Phillips had been the officer in charge of the English artillery at Minden. Lafayette did get to Richmond first, just barely, and he put up a show of strength that gave the British pause—though in truth Phillips and Arnold were much stronger than Lafayette at that time. Would they hear of this? Would their scouts learn it, their spies report it? Lafayette waited, breathless, poised. If attacked he could only retreat—and he had nowhere to go.

Abruptly General Phillips turned around and marched the other way, toward Petersburg. The situation, for the moment, had been saved. Lafayette's spies—who were efficient, for he paid them well, out of his own pocket—soon reported that Phillips had received a message from Cornwallis, who was coming north, and who had ordered Phillips to meet him at Petersburg.

Lafayette could wait a little while. No doubt Lord Cornwallis would enjoy the privilege of pouncing upon him.

The British charged that some militiamen had fired on a British flag of truce, and Phillips wrote a highhanded, imperious letter to Lafayette, demanding that something be done about this instantly, sir, and threatening dire reprisals. Lafayette replied that he would investigate.

A few days later there came a letter not from Phillips but from Benedict Arnold as second-in-command, for General Phillips was laid up with a fever. This message doubtless had to do with an exchange of prisoners or else with the alleged flag-shooting incident, but Lafayette refused to read it or even to open it. The aide who had brought it was instructed to take it back to "the English general who is at this moment commander in chief"—for Lafayette would not even pronounce the traitor's name. The aide, a captain, returned the next day. Now, he declared, General Arnold actually and literally *was* the commanding officer of the other force, for General Phillips had died. (Phillips had been dead for two days, but for reasons of their own his aides and assistants were keeping this a secret.)

Still Lafayette refused to accept the letter.

The rumor soon sped around camp that Arnold had poisoned Phillips, so as to get the command for himself. It was known that they didn't see eye to eye. And one of the ancient scandals raked up against Arnold at the time of his sellout was that on a

voyage to the West Indies he, the supercargo, had poisoned
Captain Young Ledyard of Groton, Connecticut, in order that
he could take over and sell the cargo for himself. It was certain
at least that the captain did die at sea and was buried there,
that Arnold did return from that voyage a comparatively rich
man, and that Arnold once had worked for an apothecary in
New Haven. The men didn't need to know any more.

Washington, when this little contretemps had been reported
to him, praised Lafayette for his stand. Yet that stand might well
have led to awkwardnesses and perhaps hardships for unoffend-
ing prisoners but for the fact that Arnold's tenure was to be so
short; for Cornwallis was on his way north.

Cornwallis came, bursting with confidence, for his was a san-
guine disposition. He fairly whooped with joy when he learned
that Lafayette was so close at hand and so poorly protected.

"The boy cannot escape me," he wrote to Clinton.[24]

He crowed too soon.

Chapter Sixteen

WHAT WERE THE FRENCH in America doing all this time? Nothing.

February 6, 1778, in Paris, there had been signed a treaty for
which there was no precedent—nor has there been anything
like it since—between the France of Louis XVI and the "United
States of North America," pledging both sides to eternal amity,
declaring war on Great Britain, promising that neither party
would make a separate peace, and specifically disclaiming on
the part of France any designs on "the northern part of America"—that is, Canada, of which she had so recently and so
cruelly been stripped. At the time it was thought by many
that there was something fishy about that treaty, which, from

the patriotic American point of view at least, was too good to be true. Surely France was more concerned with the struggle against Great Britain elsewhere—India, the Mediterranean, most of all the West Indies[25]—than with the struggle in the colonies of mainland America. Few believed the promise about Canada. There must be some secret clause, something that had not been made public, many muttered knowingly; and the English were quick to roil this suspicion with propaganda.[26]

Until that time the French had been giving under-the-counter aid to the rebellious colonies, chiefly through a Spanish firm, Rodrique Hortalez et Cie., located in the former Dutch embassy in the Faubourg du Temple, Paris, and operated by that amazing financier, watchmaker, harp teacher, and author of *The Barber of Seville,* Pierre Augustin Caron de Beaumarchais. Now the business was brought into the open, but it was not necessarily made more efficient.

When the Count de Rochambeau was offered command of an expeditionary force of four thousand it was proposed to send to America, he accepted, but at the same time he protested against the size of that force. He should have at least one-third of his men always held in reserve, he said. In other words, if he was expected to operate with four thousand he should be assigned six thousand. The government, in a benign mood, not only acquiesced but doubled the original stake, making it eight thousand; and eight thousand men, or very near that many, actually were assembled at Brest in the spring of 1780. There was not room for all of them and their equipment in the vessels the navy provided,[27] which were of course late; and after some weeks in cramped quarters in port, weeks that brought about a big sickness list, the wind at last became favorable, and some 5,500 troops sailed, in ten warships and thirty transports. After seventy days at sea, during which they had met with a gale (a gale that blew back into port the British fleet sent out to intercept them), a great deal of sickness, and a brush with a small British squadron off Bermuda (they had made an extreme southerly course in order to avoid the enemy), they dropped anchor at Newport, Rhode Island, July 11. The balance, some 1,500, were to follow as soon as ships could be provided.

It was a great show at Newport, which then for the first time became a fashionable village. There were processions, candles in windows, wreaths, speeches, drills, toasts, all the rest of it, with Major General William Heath personally representing George Washington.

Nobody in America ever had seen anything like these visitors. They were crack troops, the best in the world, and, cognizant that they were about to penetrate a wild, wild land, they had come with all their equipment, down to the last toothpick, the last corkscrew, and spares. They were well supplied with money, too, and it was gold.

War still was an aristocratic sport to the French, and this force glittered with ancient and honorable names—De Saint-Maine, Deux-Ponts, De Charlus, De Castine, De Noailles (Lafayette was married to a Noailles), De Laval-Montmorency. Chevaliers were hardly more than sergeants in those officers' messes, and counts, viscounts and marquises were everywhere, while there was even one duke—the Duc de Lauzun, the Don Juan of his time, who however put aside his philandering out of respect for the seriousness of the occasion.

Such supplies, too, never before had been seen, such food, so much wine. These men all had boots, and kept them polished. They were divided into four regiments. The Deux-Ponts wore white coats, the Saintonges white, purple, and green, the Bourbonnais black turned over with red and piped with cream, and the Soissonnais white with rose facings. All of them wore cocked hats—excepting the Soissonnais, who wore tall grenadier caps with white and rose-colored plumes—but the officers' hats were cocked in only two places, not three, as was the custom: they were very jaunty, and a novelty. There was also an artillery outfit, which wore coats of sky blue turned over with scarlet.

The party of Oneidas and Tuscaroras brought in to entertain the high-ranking officers at a banquet given them by General

Heath must have looked drab in the presence of these bedizened warriors. The redskins, while they were still sober, did what they said was a war dance.

It was clear that the French needed a few weeks in which to get their land legs and to assort their matériel in its proper order. The local folks loved them. Everybody was happy; but for some time nothing much was done.

Washington sent Lafayette to represent him, in talks about strategy. This seemed the most natural thing in the world to George Washington, whose contacts with Frenchmen up to this time had been on the field of battle, and who couldn't speak a word of the language; but at Newport it was not accepted as such. To them, there, Lafayette was a bit overspirited, and his insistence that the average Continental soldier was as good as any European soldier simply struck them as silly.

The meeting at Hartford helped, but not a great deal. Each side was pleased by the appearance of the other, and Washington in particular made a deep impression: his size, his dignity, his innate graciousness, enormously moved these his allies, who noted also a certain poetic sadness about him, for "He looks like a hero," Count Fersen wrote to his father from Hartford. Yet the best that that conference could do was agree that more troops were needed, and more money, for which, jointly, they applied to Versailles. Then Washington rode back—to run into the perfidy of Benedict Arnold.

That held up everything for some time, since nobody could be sure of how many men might follow Arnold, or whether in a little while there would even *be* a Continental army. Rochambeau's orders were clear. He could put himself under the command of George Washington, but not under the command of any other American military officer, and in any event his army must remain a unit that should not be broken. Washington was to be considered, and treated, as a marshal of the French army. He was. And this was gratifying to the spectators; but it did not prove anything.

There were sundry reasons why this fine French army at Newport remained inactive for almost a year. Daily, for months, Rochambeau expected his second division, and to move without this would seem folly. An answer to the appeal for more money and more equipment and more troops should be awaited. To make matters even more complicated, the Continental Congress, without having conferred with Washington, decided to appeal to France directly, and for this purpose it appointed one of Washington's few French-speaking aides, Henry Laurens. (Another, Alexander Hamilton, who still wasn't speaking to his chief, might have been a happier choice than Laurens, a pushing person, and Hamilton had asked for the job.)

So they sat down to wait, the count and the impatient commander in chief, though each of them would have preferred action. Washington knew that he could have issued a command that would set the French into motion, but he also knew that his own army was falling apart and that to move at all, in any direction, might mean to collapse. Rochambeau's orders, again, were plain. If the Continental army dissolved, he and all of his force must come back home.

All the while, day and night, in fair weather and foul, the British navy doggedly paced the waters off Point Judith. The British navy was in one of its worst periods, having been starved, cut down, neglected, while the French navy never had been better; but in this part of the world, presently at least, the British held an emphatic superiority, which they exploited to the full. Admiral Ternay and his vessels with prudence stayed in harbor; and it was patent to everybody concerned that nothing could be done without command of the coast.

Here was a stalemate, an expensive one. These magnificent Frenchmen remained in and near Newport, doing nothing, not even able to lay plans, simply being decorative. They paid in real money and they were well behaved, so they were by no means unwelcome guests; but the cause of liberty dawdled.

The British for their part did nothing either. They themselves had held Newport and much of the rest of Rhode Island during the early part of this war, but now, in the north, they were huddled only in New York City and Staten Island, though from time to time they raided in Westchester County and in New Jersey. Their one stab at the French encampment was abortive. It was to have been two-pronged, amphibious, army and navy at the same time, but when Sir Henry Clinton, leading the army, got halfway there he heard that Washington was about to attack New York City at his rear; and he whirled around and hurried back. Thus Washington's feint—for it had been nothing more—had its intended result; and in addition it led to some sarcastic remarks on the part of the stranded Admiral Arbuthnot and it marked the beginning of the feud between him and Sir Henry.

A gale early in March tossed the patrol vessels so severely that they had to put back to New York for refitting. The new French naval commander, Destouches—Ternay had recently died—took advantage of this, sending forth eight warships to Virginia in an attempt to bottle up Benedict Arnold. Washington was there at Newport to see them off, and he was made much of, feasted, given a salute of thirteen guns—for the French had plenty of powder—but nothing came of this sally, and the situation remained the same.

Washington several times pressed upon Rochambeau the suggestion that he combine forces with the Spanish in the West Indies and make an attack upon Georgia, which might be won back from the British, thereby gaining Florida as well; but Rochambeau, who knew the Spaniards better than Washington did, shook a sad head. Spain was at war with Great Britain, yes, but reluctantly, only at the insistence of France, and the Spanish admiral was a stickler for orders and could never be persuaded that by conquering Georgia, Florida might be regained. It wasn't even worth trying, Rochambeau said.

May 8 a French frigate put in to Boston with a distinguished company and some interesting news. Besides the new admiral, De Barras, she brought back Rochambeau's own son, a colonel, who had been sent to France with his father's and Washington's request for more men and more money. The men were denied. Not only would the French court not send the fifteen thousand asked for but it had been decided not even to send the fifteen hundred who made up Rochambeau's long-awaited second division. It was thought that Washington ought to raise his own men; and indeed, the Continental army was at all times shamefully small for a country that claimed a population of three million. The French crown realized that money was needed for this purpose, and the sum of six million gold livres was sent with young Rochambeau—not as a loan but as an out-and-out gift. That was good. It did serve to keep the Continental army together a little longer and to make it somewhat less disheveled, though it did little to enlarge it.

France was the only nation even to think about giving the United States money. The Netherlands would furnish ten million livres, but only on the condition that King Louis XVI himself underwrite the loan. The French were working on this. There was hope.

The best part of the news that Colonel Rochambeau brought, however, was not written. It was confidential, for the two commanders.

The French Admiral de Grasse was assembling a mighty fleet at Brest, and he would sail soon for the West Indies. Included in his orders was one that he sail to the mainland of North America some time before the summer was out and see if he could do anything to help the Continentals and the French expedition in Rhode Island.

This called for a conference, and Washington and Rochambeau met again officially and formally—this time at Wethersfield, Connecticut, for the state legislature was meeting at Hartford, where there would be no accommodations. It was ordinarily a three-day trip, but Washington rode the forty-three miles between Fishkill and Morgan's Tavern on May 18 and was in Wethersfield, just south of Hartford, the next day. He was put up at the home of Joseph Webb. In the morning he went to church with that stout patriot, Governor Jonathan Trumbull, the original Brother Jonathan.[28] The text was,

"Blessed are the poor in spirit, for theirs is the kingdom of Heaven." Early Monday Washington rode up to Hartford to greet and ride back with Rochambeau and his staff.

They agreed that for the present there was little they could do. Everything depended upon De Grasse—when he came, where he came, *if* he came. They did decide, there in Wethersfield, that New York City was the logical place to hit, provided that De Grasse sailed that far north. However, De Grasse himself might object to this, for the French warships generally drew more water than did the British, and the French feared that they might have trouble crossing the bar into New York harbor, whereas Chesapeake Bay was perfectly safe. De Barras was not there to give his own opinion of this, to the disappointment of Washington, who had looked forward to meeting the newly arrived admiral. The patrols had been making threatening gestures, and De Barras thought that he ought to stay with his charges at Newport.

Such was the situation at the opening of the long summer of 1781.

Chapter Seventeen

As IF THE COMBINED forces were not enough, a few days after the British had made their junction at Petersburg a new batch of reinforcements, two freshly-out regiments of redcoats and two battalions of Anspachers, arrived at Portsmouth, Virginia, where Cornwallis scooped them up.

Cornwallis now had a total of about 7,200 men, including the two swift mounted outfits, Simcoe's and Tarleton's, for whom this countryside might have been made. Lafayette, militia and all, numbered only about 2,000. He could not think of opposing the British directly. On the other hand, as he wrote to Washington, if he simply ran away from the enemy the Vir-

ginians would think that he was about to abandon their state
and they would cease entirely to enlist. He proposed, then, to
keep close, but not too close, and he would be especially leery
of "their immense and excellent body of horse, whom the militia
fear as they would so many wild beasts." Lafayette himself had
only forty dragoons. "I am not strong enough even to get
beaten," he wrote plaintively.

Where was Wayne? Wayne and up to one thousand Pennsylvania regulars had been promised him, and they should have
been here before this. Supply problems—but Lafayette could
not know this—had held them up. Also, there had been a brief
recurrence of the mutiny. The day before they were to march,
while they had formed for their last parade, men began to cry
that they would not take a step out of the state until they'd been
paid. Wayne, an old hand at mutinies by this time, acted with
dispatch. He hauled one man, the loudest, out of each of the
six battalions. He had the six taken to the middle of a field,
where their arms were tied before them, their faces were
masked, and they were forced to kneel. He told off a large firing
squad to shoot them in the back. Two were pardoned at the
last moment, but the other four were all but ripped apart by
so many heavy musket balls fired at such close range. They
must have made a messy sight as they lay there in a heap, all
blood and shredded flesh, attracting flies. The whole outfit—it
numbered only about eight hundred men, not the thousand
Wayne had promised—was made to march in single file, and
slowly, past this. The next morning, "mute as fish," they started
south.

Richmond was hardly any longer a prize, being little more
than a ghost town, for Arnold's men had spent two busy days,
earlier in the year, taking it apart. At one time Richmond had
been a storage place for patriot supplies, but these had been
moved. The legislature too had been moved. It was no longer
at Williamsburg, or temporarily at Richmond, but was now
farther west, at Charlottesville, whither Cornwallis sent the
spectacular Tarleton.

On the way, his body of horse came upon twelve unguarded wagonloads of clothing marked for Greene's army in North Carolina. They burned these.

They moved so fast that they almost surprised the Assembly in the middle of a session. Only the quick thinking and fast riding of one Captain John Jouett, who lived on the line of march and saw them coming and leaped on his horse and beat them into town, saved the solons, a few of whom were captured anyway.[29] The British, literally, were coming in one end of the town while the legislators were running out of the other, hardly an edifying spectacle. The British burned a lot of tobacco, exploded a lot of gunpowder, and destroyed still more clothing meant for Greene, without losing a man. Captain McLeod rode over the Secretary's Ford and started up to Monticello, but the governor already had been warned and had slipped out by a garden gate, on foot.

A week later Thomas Jefferson, whose two-year term had expired, ceased to be governor. There were those among his adorers—of whom he had many in Virginia, though he was not well known in the other states—who had urged him to run for re-election. He decided against this, and it was as well that he did, for almost certainly he would have been beaten. The very things that made the sage of Monticello a great peacetime executive made him a poor wartime governor. He was a strict constitutionalist at a time when the constitution should not have been held sacred. He wouldn't make a swift decision or take big chances. He had no military imagination, no military foresight. Despite repeated warnings, Virginia, the richest state of them all, had been unprepared for invasion. At first she had not even tried to fight back, when Benedict Arnold had everything his own way; and this was humiliating. There were murmurs that Jefferson was slow, that he was timid, hesitant. A decisive man was needed. Some said that the first governor, Patrick Henry (Jefferson was the second), should be called out of retirement and invested with extraordinary powers: the word "dictator" often was used, and in hope rather than in fear. An investigation into the dying administration was voted, though for lack of time it was never held. There was even talk of impeachment proceedings. So it was generally agreed, except by his most fanatical admirers, that Thomas Jefferson did well when he decided not to run again.

His successor, Thomas Nelson, Jr., a conservative planter, was head of the Virginia militia and a man of great energy. The Assembly did invest him with extraordinary powers, but almost certainly Nelson would have taken those powers anyway. For he was that kind of man; he got things done. There was nothing lethargic now about the capital, which incidentally had been moved to Staunton, still farther west.

Cornwallis did take the trouble to march through Richmond, but that was only after he had given up hope of preventing Lafayette from joining Anthony Wayne. If Cornwallis was indeed a modern Hannibal, then Lafayette was his Quintus Fabius. The Frenchman would duck and feint, disappear, reappear, disperse his forces, draw them together again. He was a gadfly, a pest, devilishly ingenious, appallingly persistent, and he refused to be swatted.

The union with Wayne was effected June 10, and this, together with certain other reinforcements in the form of small clumps of militia, brought Lafayette's force up to about four thousand. He would still have to be cagey, but now at least he might seize a chance to strike here and there, to threaten, to snap.

Just at this time, too, Lord Cornwallis began to fall back, east, toward the sea. Immediately and with elation Lafayette went after him, pressing him. To the world it might look as though Cornwallis was in retreat before a belligerent Frenchman. Lafayette knew that this was not so, but the appearance in itself, just at this time when the new nation sought recognition, could be important.

At Spencer's Ordinary, a tavern midway between the Chickahominy and the York, west of Williamsburg, a party of patriots under Colonel Richard Butler of Pennsylvania—most of them were Pennsylvanians—early on the morning of June 26 suddenly fell upon a party of mounted Jägers and Queen's Rangers under Simcoe. The fight that followed was a confused affair, and the patriots, who had marched all night to cut off this foraging party, eventually were driven from the field. But they had behaved well, and the British-Hessian casualties were the greater.

Cornwallis continued to move toward the coast, and a jubilant Marquis de Lafayette continued to follow him.

Chapter Eighteen

BESIDES THE GAME of Stealing Generals, they also played the game of Stealing Mail, often with startling results. The British generally had the advantage in this latter sport, and that for a variety of reasons.

There was no regular postal system in the country. Before the war, letters often went by sea—or at least by water—as the roads were impassable for part of each year and abominable all the year around. For instance, it was cheaper, safer, and in most cases took less time for a man in New York writing to a man in Philadelphia to send his letter by schooner around Cape May. The same was true of Boston and New York. And nobody even thought of going from the middle or eastern states to the southern states by land. But the coming of war had made all coasting dangerous where it was even possible.

In addition, many of the Continental military movements were far inland, since the British denied their enemy the use of the coast.

The British had been much better equipped with horses in the first place. Their couriers were a part of their army, subject to military discipline. It was not so in the Continental army, which could not afford to raise and train such a service but had to depend upon civilian riders, who were more likely to be robbed—or bribed. A great many patriot letters and dispatches, some of the greatest importance, went astray or fell into the eager hands of the British.

Early in the conflict that incorrigible applecart-upsetter, John Adams, a delegate to the Second Continental Congress which was just about to adopt the Declaration of Independence, sent a letter from Philadelphia to a friend in Boston, in which, in a style "more energetic than elegant,"[30] he gave his opinion of some of his associates. That letter never got to Boston. It was intercepted by the British at Newport, quite by chance, and the British, whooping with delight, published it. There is no way of calculating how much damage this did, but it was considerable.

Washington was a prodigious letter writer, and though he could be careful in his official correspondence, he often let himself go in personal epistles, so that he more than any other suffered from this game. He wrote to Benjamin Harrison and to Lund Washington in Virginia, and these letters got to Sir Henry Clinton—or rather, to that ardent young New York loyalist, Colonel James De Lancey, who had succeeded John André as head of the British Intelligence service in America, and who saw to it that Rochambeau in Newport got copies of them. For Rochambeau was criticized in these letters for his lack of action at Newport. Hurt, Rochambeau wrote to Washington, who in reply pointed out that these were private opinions privately expressed and not in any way official, and that, besides, he still thought that way. Nothing came of the incident. It was the nearest that these two ever came to a quarrel, and it was not very close.

Unabashed, Washington soon afterward wrote to Lafayette in Virginia that it was the current thinking of the high command of both armies, French and Continental, that New York should be attacked, if only in order to relieve the pressure on Virginia. In that same sack of mail, sent by ordinary public courier, was a letter from the Marquis de Chastellux to his friend De la Luzerne, the French ambassador at Philadelphia.

In New Jersey, an enterprising young man named John Moody, who specialized in this sort of theft, held up the public courier and sent the sack to New York.

The Chastellux letter De Lancey gleefully translated, but he forwarded the original to Rochambeau, about whom the writer had expressed some unflattering thoughts. There was no duel; but this sort of thing did not help.

The Moody haul was valuable largely because of the Washington letter, for which a delighted Sir Henry Clinton paid two hundred guineas.

Yet—after his first flush of elation Sir Henry began to be troubled about that letter, wondering whether it wasn't, after all, a ruse?

The letter was dated May 31, ten days after the Wethersfield conference. Two days before that, Washington had written the same thing to General John Sullivan, who had quit the army and was in Congress at Philadelphia, a member from New Hampshire. This letter too was stolen, though it reached Clinton a little after the other, perhaps because of haggling on the part of the thief.

At about the same time an intercepted letter from a high-ranking French officer to a friend in Philadelphia said the same thing all over again.

Sir Henry was a man who scared easily. Now suddenly he was convinced that this whole thing was a plot to make him think that the damned rebels were going to strike at Virginia while he hugged his troops in New York. Three letters all at once like that—it wasn't natural. Well, he'd fool 'em! Cornwallis's action in marching into Virginia had astounded the British commander in chief, for it was done "without my approbation, and very contrary to my wishes and intentions."[31] Now, all but hearing the siege guns, he sat down and wrote to Cornwallis orders to proceed to the coast of Virginia, near the capes, and pick out that naval station site they had talked about. At the same time, and while he was there, Cornwallis was to send, immediately, three thousand of his best troops to New York.

Only a few weeks before, Clinton had sent fifteen hundred reinforcements to Virginia. Now he was demanding 3,000 back.

The game of Stealing Mail had recoiled upon the thief.

Chapter Nineteen

GEORGE WASHINGTON in public always was impassive, but the members of his official "family" knew that he had a short temper: he was thin-skinned, very touchy about the respect due to him and to his rank. Yet he could cool quickly, for he had a heap of common sense. He had squabbled in this way once—the details are lost—with Nathanael Greene, ordinarily a very good-natured man. This had long since been patched up. Washington held no grudge. He would gladly, if only for the sake of the cause, send Greene supplies in North Carolina, but for two reasons he could not do so: (1) Because of the activity of Cornwallis in Virginia—Arnold had been recalled by this time—any supplies sent would not be likely to get through. (2) He had no supplies to send anyway.

And Greene needed them so desperately! His men suffered; and he too suffered, watching them.

He was facing a different fencer now, on the same old strip. When Cornwallis took the step that was to prove fatal, he possibly hoped that Greene could be enticed into following him into Virginia. This Greene had no intention of doing. The British left in the Carolinas even after the departure of Cornwallis numbered about two and a half times as many men as Greene could possibly put into the field at one time, but they were scattered through no fewer than ten farflung posts. It was Nathanael Greene's plan, simply, to take those posts one by one. However, he had no objection to meeting Lord Rawdon in an open fight first. If Rawdon's force was defeated, then the whole job would be easier.

This Rawdon—the title was only a courtesy one—was but twenty-six years old, but he had seen a lot of service. He had been at Lexington and at Concord. A lieutenant in his teens, when his captain was killed at Bunker Hill he had taken command of his company and led it back into the fray. He had been on Long Island, on the Brandywine, at Germantown, at Monmouth. He had seen at least as much action as had Greene himself, a man twice his age.

Rawdon had dash, but he also had imagination: he was no copybook general. He was tall and thin, with dark hair, and an incredibly homely but somehow pleasing face.[32]

Just now Rawdon was at Camden, which Greene approached, eight months to the day after Cornwallis had smashed Gates's army there.

Greene paused at a wooded rise called Hobkirk's Hill. This was about a mile and a half north of Camden, which itself was a naturally strong position, protected as it was by two streams. Probably Greene wished to wait for some of his brilliant but erratic militia brigadiers to catch up with him—something that they never did—but Rawdon saw no reason to wait. Rawdon came out swinging.

It was a slam-bang battle. The Continentals had been surprised at breakfast, but they assembled quickly, neatly, and faced the British in a long heavy line. They outnumbered the British, about twelve hundred to nine hundred.[33] Their position was sound. If they waited there for the attack they might well smash it. But Greene saw a chance to extend them and to bear-hug the British, who were coming in on a narrow line. He caused his flanks to be thrown out, while Colonel Washington, hidden behind a hill as usual, was to circle clear around to the rear of the British. Greene ordered a charge.

Against a slow-witted British commander, this highly unorthodox move might have succeeded; but Rawdon saw the trick instantly and countered it by bringing up his second line, which he spread. From then on it was simply toe to toe. The patriots, or some of them, broke. These were regulars—for the battle plan on the part of Greene was the opposite to Cowpens, to Guilford Courthouse: Greene here had his regulars in the first line, his militia behind.

It was a Maryland outfit that broke. The men had seen some of their best officers down, and they began to back away. There was no rout; but their colonel decided to march them back in order to reassemble them.[34] It *looked* like a retreat. And the British came in running.

Colonel Washington? His cavalry had been whittled down by operations, and he had today only eighty-seven men—but only *fifty-six* horses. Even so, he swung clear around to the rear of the enemy. It proved to be a long swing, because of the nature of the terrain, and Washington came up far to the rear, among the camp followers of the British army[35]—sutlers, laundresses, whores, the usual riffraff, protected by a guard that could hardly have been formidable: prized soldiers are seldom given such an assignment. Colonel Washington readily seized this mixed, unappetizing group, and with the thought that the battle was the patriots' anyway began to claim prisoners. When he learned that the battle was going the other way he still tried to keep some of those prisoners, it is hard to see why.

Colonel Washington, then, with his handful, a prisoner behind every horseman, charged straight through the British lines from behind. As was so often the case with this detachment, the stroke was so unexpected that it did not fail. Throwing off prisoners right and left, as they saw how serious was the situation, Washington's men at least did help to save the three poor small patriot artillery pieces that had been threatened.

The field was lost. But it was no crushing defeat. The patriots brought in their wounded and buried their dead. They were pursued, but not far. The British had had enough. The Americans never really broke, never panicked, and fought a determined and steady rear-guard action, so that the British, though they *had* won the field, lost badly in men—more than the patriots, more than they could afford.

Nathanael Greene was heartbroken, but he needn't have been. It was another loss chalked up against his record, but he could spare it.

It was a victory for Lord Rawdon, his first independent field command. Covered quite properly with glory, he soon went back to England, for his health was poor.

And Greene sighed and prepared to go on slugging.

Chapter Twenty

THE FOURTH OF JULY in that year 1781—at least at Tyree's Plantation, twenty miles northwest of Williamsburg, Virginia, where Lafayette and his men were encamped—started out wet, rainy, and that could have been a bad sign; but by midmorning it began to clear. The troops made much of this, the nation's fifth Independence Day. There was a dress parade, a *feu de joie,* an extra rum-ration all around, and a banquet that the marquis gave to his officers.

It looked as though the "retreat" might have come to an end. The British had taken up quarters in Williamsburg, and the Americans had prudently halted short of that town to wait and see what the "retreaters" would do next.

Things were going as well as could be expected, possibly even somewhat better. "Since I am first in command," the marquis had complained in a letter to General Greene, "I become a great coward." He belittled himself. In fact he was doing a wonderful job, using everything that he had, resisting every impulse to dash in. No longer was he fighting "this kind of runaway war that I most heartily detest." If he had not truly taken the offensive, he *seemed* to have done so; and this could be important at a time when there were rumors that arbitrators in Vienna were about to propose an end to the war and local sporting men were laying five to one that peace would be declared before the end of the year. A show of strength might bring better terms in Vienna.

The weather was equable. The shirts had come from Baltimore. Desertions were, comparatively, trifling; and there was no immediate hint of mutiny. Congress was making all sorts of appropriations; and while it was true that these came in the form of depreciated Continental notes—the ratio to gold was 1,000 to 1 now—it did keep the men at the commissary busy moving that much paper from place to place. The news from France was better, much better. The news from the south was bad; yet Lafayette, like everybody else who knew him, had great confidence in Nathanael Greene.

The marquis was not strong enough to attack Cornwallis, but he was well fitted out for snapping at Cornwallis's heels. The runaway days were over, he hoped.

The two enemies Lafayette most feared were smallpox and the harvest. While in the Carolinas malaria had been the fiercest foe Rawdon and Greene had to combat, in tidewater Virginia that summer it was not rampant. Neither was smallpox, though that dread disease might put in an appearance at any time. As for the harvest, it would strip him of half his army when it did come—and it *would* come. For all the new emergency laws and for all the election—and the stern new governor, Nelson, was right with him, right at the same banquet table— the Virginia militia would vanish like snow upon the desert's dusty face as soon as ever the time came for the men to get in their crops.

Meanwhile, however, things were going well enough.

And it was as he reflected on this that they brought the marquis news that the British were clearing out of Williamsburg.

Oh, they were not coming toward him! They were not about to attack. It was southeast, not west, that they were making their way; and from the gist of Lafayette's intelligence this could only mean that they were going to Portsmouth. Why Portsmouth, a less comfortable, less salubrious place than Williamsburg, he could not see—for good though his spy organization was it could hardly be expected to tell him about Cornwallis's orders to survey for a naval base—but clearly, at least, the British were about to jump the James.

Why not attack them when they were half or somewhat more than half across? Why not sweep down upon them and erase the rear guard? Cornwallis was not taking him, Lafayette, seriously. Cornwallis would not expect such a movement.

Here the marquis was mistaken. Cornwallis was laying his plans with exactly that in mind; for the noble lord, like any good chess player, like a good swordsman, sought always to keep one thought ahead of his opponent. The French lad, belying his reputation for rashness, had been a model of discretion; but could he keep that up? Could he resist rushing into the kind of trap that Cornwallis would set for him?

Lafayette, enraptured at the thought that he would have some action at last, even though it would be less than a pitched battle, ordered camp struck and a march southeast begun early the next morning.

The afternoon of the sixth, the patriots' advance guard under Anthony Wayne came upon what it took to be the rear guard of the British. All the rest of the British army, it was assumed —and, from every evidence of the eyes, *logically* assumed— already had crossed the river.

This was at a place called Green Spring Farm, level, open ground, most of it, but the portion that bordered the river was a morass, a forest, with only a few narrow paths leading to the shore.

A few units of Simcoe's Rangers in fact had crossed the James to its south bank, where they spread out, making a show of numbers in order to deceive any possible long-range scouts. All the others were hidden in the swamp. And they were faced *away from* the river, and deployed for battle.

The scattered posts that Wayne took to be the rear guard

really was a van. He drove them in, but the fighting was brisk, stubborn. Even Wayne had to stop and catch his breath—and save his life.

The very nature of the terrain, which might have been designed for use as a snare, should have warned Wayne to use caution; but caution was foreign to his soul.

Cornwallis could have swarmed out of his cover right then and there—and Wayne and his 400-odd regulars would have been lost. But Cornwallis was greedy. He wanted the greater part of the whole patriot army. With the force he had on hand he could gulp this like a tidbit; which is what he meant to do.

Lafayette obliged, bringing up about twelve hundred men, leaving behind only his militia, though he himself remained on a high place in the rear in order to have a better look, through a glass, at those loyalists on the other side of the river. Lafayette was sniffing trouble. And soon he found that he had it. After a study of those forces beyond the James he sent word to Wayne to withdraw immediately—but carefully.

It was too late. Cornwallis already had started to spring the trap.

His men emerged from the forest; so that even Wayne, no intellectual giant, could see what was happening.

Wayne did an extraordinary thing, though probably it was the only thing that could have saved his men. He ordered—*a charge!*

It was not much of a charge. It wasn't meant to be. But it did take the British completely by surprise and it did disturb for a little while their previously perfect formation. The counter-attack was not prompt.

Wayne's men fell back slowly, shooting. They showed a commendable coolness and courage, but it was not these qualities that save them—it was the coming of darkness. There would be no moon that night, and the clouds were thick, dark, low. Even half an hour more of daylight, Cornwallis was to report to his superior, "would probably have given us the greater part of the corps."

The patriots lost their two small field guns, for the horses to pull them away were killed; but these guns had been spiked in time. The patriots' casualties were 145, those of the British 75.

It had been a damned close thing.

Chapter Twenty-one

EVEN THE COMMANDER in chief felt discouragement that summer, though he was able to keep the feeling to himself. After six years of unremitting warfare, six years in which he had never even glimpsed his own beloved Mount Vernon, years of worry and waste, of frustration, humiliation, he seemed to be even further than ever from victory, indeed to be teetering on the very verge of catastrophe.

Everything depended upon word from France or from De Grasse in the West Indies. If Washington could hold out until that word came, *and* if the word was good, it might yet be possible to do something before the summer was out.

The two armies were side-by-side at last. Newport was a charming place, as all of the Frenchmen agreed, but after eleven months of it they were glad to go elsewhere, anywhere. The best army in the world, as with some justice they rated themselves, was doing nothing, getting nowhere. In consequence, tempers were short, complaints loud.

Washington and Rochambeau, who agreed on most things, were agreed that New York would be the right place to hit, provided that De Grasse and his fleet appeared off Sandy Hook, though Rochambeau was not convinced that such an attack would be practical just now. They decided that the least they could do was get together at some place from which a descent upon the city could be organized.

The four foot-regiments left Newport on June 9 and went by boat to Providence, which they quit, a regiment a day, June 18, 19, 20, and 21, marching about fifteen miles apart.

Connecticut never had seen anything like this. Plainfield . . . Canterbury . . . Windham . . . Bolton . . . then Hartford, where they paused a few days to rest and to repair their wagons. Their colorful uniforms, their bright trappings, their discipline, won them oh's and ah's all along the line of march. Their behavior was impeccable. Thousands cheered them. They were showered with flowers. Farmers lent them oxen, and the owners of cider mills freely slaked their thirst. Those were four famous days in the life of each town and village. Farmington . . . Southington . . . Newtown . . . Ridgefield . . . then into New York State: Bedford and North Castle to White Plains, the camp.

About half of the officers—the estimate is Rochambeau's own —turned their horses over to servants and walked the whole distance at the head of their men, just for the exercise.

You don't often see counts and marquises trudging past your door by the dozen.

A little farther south at the same time passed the Duc de Lauzun's legion of horse and foot, which had been stationed not at Newport but, for reasons of forage for the horses, at Lebanon, Connecticut. It proceeded from there by way of Colchester, Middletown, Wallingford, Oxford, North Stratford, and Bedford, reaching White Plains at the same time as the larger body. It consisted of three hundred cavalry and three hundred mixed infantry and artillery, and it was if possible even more resplendent than those who marched farther north. The duke's cavalrymen were dressed as hussars—sky-blue jackets with bright yellow cuffs, pelisses of the same color edged with black fur and trimmed with white braid, high, black felt hussar bonnets bordered with gold galloon and decorated with white fleur-de-lis and with white plumes, yellow breeches trimmed with white braid in front, and hussar boots that had white braid tops. Their sabretaches were of blue cloth with the King's cipher in yellow and with a border of black; their buttons were white, their belts yellow and sky blue; all straps were of white buffalo.

The artillerists and infantry in this legion were similarly attired, except that they wore yellow buttons, red breeches, white gaiters, and cocked hats.

These were the rank and file. The officers were more giddily arrayed.[36]

Connecticut couldn't get enough of it. Often whole families would ride ahead at night and watch the troops pass through a second or even a third town. Aside from the color and the exquisite discipline it was the musicians, who played indefatigably for each town and village, who made the most talk. In such soldiers as the peasantry had seen before, the militia or the Continental troops that might have been stationed or passed through there, the only musical instruments were a few drums and a few sad fifes; but these glittering foreigners had all sorts of strange devices never before seen in that countryside—horns, bassoons, oboes, clarinets. They could not only beat time for marching, they could even play music—and did.

> Malbrouk s'en va-t-en guerre,
>   Mironton, mironton, mirontaine!
> Malbrouk s'en va-t-en guerre,
>   Nul sait quand reviendra!

Some of them sang, and all of them smiled. Dust or dirt or mud, they tramped along in perfect order, beaming.

> Il reviendra z'à pâques—
>   Mironton, mironton, mirontaine . . .
>   Ou la Trinité.

Two things struck the Frenchmen forcibly. One was the cheerfulness, the kindliness with which they were received, the welcome that shone bright in every face. As soldiers they were accustomed to sour looks rather than smiles. To the populace of the average European town, military visitors meant only arrogance, insult, drunkness, theft; but these people in Connecticut clearly were entertained.

The other thing that impressed the French—and impressed them even more deeply than had the friendliness of the inhabitants—was the country itself. They never had seen anything like it. Where were the clipped hedgerows, where the stately files of aspen, the roads so straight, so flat? Where were the canals? This place was *sauvage*. It was a wilderness; and any town or landscape in continental Europe compared with it would have seemed a park, like so many toys in a Bavarian dollmaker's shop. Connecticut not without reason esteemed itself pretty civilized as things in America went. Certainly it was more thickly settled and had straighter roads and better kept fields and orchards than anything western New York or western Pennsylvania or the back regions of Virginia and Georgia and the Carolinas could show. But to the marching Frenchmen it was a wilderness, and fascinating as such. They gasped, goggle-eyed, at the great distances, the wide streams, the forests so dark and ominous. They kept looking around for red Indians, very few of whom appeared.

Sightseeing aside, that movement of men was a military triumph, a testimonial to French organization. More than 4,500 soldiers had taken themselves 220 miles in eleven days, without a single straggler.

In and around White Plains and Dobbs Ferry the two armies regarded one another, and for the most part they seemed pleased with what they saw. The Americans were downright dazzled by the colors and accouterments, as folks in Connecticut and Rhode Island had been, and they were envious of the fine equipment, as well they might be. The French were hardly speechless in admiration of the *appearance* of the patriot troops—the Americans had no uniforms and wore anything they could get, as like as not a much-patched hunting shirt—but they were amazed to learn that the Americans behaved in many ways like real soldiers, that they drilled and marched well, that they carried no scalping knives or tomahawks, and that they were so stoical about what they ate, what they could live on, perforce. This was the rank and file. The French officers were scandalized by the table the Americans set. There were sundry inter-mess visits and a large formal dinner given by Washington in his own tent. After each of these, there would be among the French careful, behind-the-hand, whispered criticisms. *Ah, oui, messieurs,* the food had been sound enough, if not properly cooked, and there had been plenty of it, but—it was all put on the table at the same time! *Mon Dieu,* what kind of barbarian way to eat was that?

Washington had been doing a great deal of scouting in the spiked environs of New York City, probing for soft spots, none of which he had found. Now, with his allies by his side, he started what evidently had been meant to be a real thrust at Kingsbridge, though because it was so easily repulsed it was written down, in the accepted military manner, as a reconnaissance in force. It did serve to convince both Washington and Rochambeau that unless De Grasse came here with an overwhelming force of foot in addition to his vessels it would be foolhardy to attack New York. To Washington this was heart-killing, but it had to be faced. Clinton, who had just received reinforcements—from abroad, not from Virginia—had more than fourteen thousand men in New York City: he might have had as many as sixteen thousand. Rochambeau and Washington between them had fewer than ten thousand.

So, once again, there was nothing to do but sit down and wait.

When word did come from Admiral de Grasse, August 14, it came by way of De Barras at Newport, having reached him by fast frigate from Santo Domingo. And it was clear. It was unequivocal. De Grasse with a huge fleet already was on his way toward the mainland of North America. He had upwards of three thousand regular French troops with him. He also had four million livres, in gold. He would anchor off the Virginia capes very soon. He could only stay until October 15, for his presence in the West Indies was imperative, but until that time he would be glad to do anything he could.

Washington went into action.

Chapter Twenty-two

"THE ARMY WILL HOLD ITSELF in the most perfect readiness to move at the shortest notice," was the way his general orders started the next morning, August 15.

He appointed Heath, his top-ranking major general and probably the best man for the job anyway, to the command of West Point and the surrounding Highlands in his own, Washington's, absence.

For the commander in chief was going south in person. He wouldn't miss a chance like this.

He wrote a letter to Admiral de Grasse and entrusted this to Brigadier General the Chevalier Louis Le Bèque de Presle du Portail, a taciturn, aloof, unpleasant man, but an expert military engineer, whom Washington now sent south to survey the site and to confer with De Grasse.[37]

He arranged for preparations for a large and seemingly semi-permanent camp near Elizabethtown, New Jersey. This would make it look as though he was thinking of shifting the bulk of his army there, to attack New York by way of Staten Island. In this same connection he arranged to have inquiries made concerning the purchase, impressment, or charter of all the boats and pontoons in that vicinity.

He stimulated—or simulated—inquiries about the possible price of a whole battery of huge baking ovens similar to the one already ordered built for the French army at Chatham, New Jersey. This, again, was to give the look of a move to New Jersey, and a stay there.

He wrote to Lafayette.

HEAD QUARTERS, DOBB'S FERRY, August 15, 1781.
MY DEAR MARQUIS: I have recd. your letters of the 26th. and 30th. ulto. and 1st. Inst. I cannot learn that any troops have yet arrived at New York from Virginia. A fleet of 20 sail came in last Saturday with troops, but they are said to be Hessian Recruits from Europe.

The Concorde Frigate is arrived at Newport from Count de Grasse. He was to leave St. Domingo the 3rd. of this month with a Fleet of between 25 and 29 sail of the line and a considerable Body of land forces. His destination is immediately for the Chesapeak. So that he will either be there by the time this reaches you, or you look for him every moment. Under these circumstances, whether the enemy remain in full force, or whether they have only a detachment left, you will immediately take such a position as will best enable you to prevent their sudden retreat thro' North Carolina, which I presume they will attempt the instant they perceive so formidable an Armament. Should General Wayne with the troops destined for South Carolina still remain in the neighborhood of James River and the enemy should have made no detachment to the southward, you will detain those troops untill you hear from me again, and inform Genl. Greene of the cause of their delay. If Wayne should have marched, and should have gained any considerable distance, I would not have him halted.

You shall hear further from me as soon as I have concerted plans and formed dispositions for sending a reinforcement from hence. In the mean time I have only to recommend a continuation of that prudence and good conduct which you have manifested thro' the whole of your Campaign. You will be particularly careful to conceal the expected arrival of the Count, because if the enemy are not apprised of it, they will stay on board their transports in the Bay, which will be the luckiest Circumstance in the World.

You will take measures for opening a communication with Count de Grasse the moment he arrives, and will concert measures with him for making the best uses of your joint forces untill you receive aid from this quarter. I am &c.

P.S. I would not wish you to call out a large body of Militia upon this occasion, but rather keep those you have compact and ready for service.

There were two dismaying features in the letter from De Barras. One was the announcement on the part of De Grasse that he could not linger in continental waters later than October 15, which gave them two months and one day in which to provision and supply two armies, march them and their heavy siege trains for almost five hundred miles, part of the way obliquely past an established and much stronger enemy, make contact with the French navy, lay out investing trenches, and flush from his hole one of the wiliest-fox generals in the world.

The other unsettling bit of news was the announcement on the part of De Barras himself that he did not think he would go south and join De Grasse: on the contrary, he thought he would go north and see what pickings might present themselves off Newfoundland. Since his was an independent command, De Barras had every right to do this. He might get some easy prize money in that direction, for with his eight warships he was surely bigger than anything Great Britain would have in those waters. On the other hand, if he joined De Grasse, who was his superior, it would be all work and no glory; for who ever hears of the second-in-command? Clearly then, every effort should be made to get De Barras to change his mind. Rochambeau and Washington were agreed on this, as they were agreed on almost everything, working together well. Each sat down and wrote an imploring letter to the admiral at Newport, who unexpectedly and most graciously consented to go to the Virginia capes instead of Newfoundland. More, he would carry their siege train for them.

Cornwallis, accompanied by engineers, had taken a good long look at Old Point Comfort, which he decided was not a desirable site for a navy station. He quit Portsmouth, then, and went over to the narrow peninsula of York, and from there, where he made his headquarters, he sent a subsidiary force across the York River—it is about a mile wide at this point, its mouth— to occupy another peninsula, Gloucester. Assuming the sea behind him to be held by the enemy, he was not just in one trap, he was in two.

The watchful Lafayette couldn't have been better pleased. He called in Weedon, Muhlenberg, Steuben, and Wayne, and made his own camp on the Pamunkey near Williamsburg, sending Wayne to Cabin Point on the James, thus effectively bottling up Lord Cornwallis and the whole British army in Virginia. Washington had written him that he could keep Wayne, who had been about to be transferred to Greene's army in the Carolinas.

Washington in the north agreed to leave Heath about three thousand troops, most of them New Englanders. This would be little enough if Sir Henry Clinton, to counter the stab at Virginia, gathered all his strength and threw himself upon West Point, as he might be expected to do. But Washington was desperate. The force he would take with him numbered hardly more than two thousand, which made it less than half the size of the French force. It was the cream of his army, such as that was, and consisted of Colonel Alexander Scammell's four hundred light-infantry troops, a Rhode Island regiment that was rated one of the best in the service, Hazen's "Canadians," two New York Continental line regiments, sundry small groups of light cavalry from New York and Connecticut, Colonel John Lamb's artillery regiment, and a smattering of sappers, miners, engineers.

This force, then, met with the French army at King's Ferry about eight miles below Peekskill on the Hudson River, August 19, a day of pouring rain. At two o'clock the next morning the crossing was started, Washington being one of the first to go over.

Washington took up his headquarters in a house of black memory, the mansion near Haverstraw that belonged to the loyalist jurist William Smith and was presently occupied by his brother, Joshua Hett Smith, who a little while ago had been exonerated (as had Varick and Franks) of any guilt in the Benedict Arnold affair. Joshua Smith, the court had held, as had the public, was stupid, hoodwinked, rather than a conspirator. It was in this very house that John André had conferred at such length with Benedict Arnold. It was here that André had spent the night; and it was from here—for the place commanded a beautiful view of the river—that the next morning he had seen H. M. S. *Vulture* driven downstream by the guns at Teller's Point, which driving-off meant that the young man would have to return to town by land. "Treason House" it was already being called by the neighbors. However, it was ideal for Washington's present purpose. He invited Rochambeau there for breakfast the morning of August 21.

It was late on the twenty-second before the more heavily equipped French got their last men and their last guns across the river, and then both armies rested for a little while, during which time supplies were brought up from behind and elaborately rigged rumors were blown out ahead. The truth is that while the French had no opinion on this subject, and didn't care, most of the Americans, including most or even all of the officers, still firmly believed that they were about to attack New York City, the only dissension being as to whether this would be done by way of Staten Island or by way of Paulus Hook.[38] If *they* believed that, it was quitely likely that the British would.

August 29, at dawn, they started south.

Chapter Twenty-three

THOSE VETERAN Continentals—there weren't many of them left —who had been in the war from the beginning: *they* knew New Jersey very well indeed, for they had marched back and forth across that state many a time, usually in retreat. It was no novelty to them. They were more interested in making bets as to whether their destination was going to be Paulus Hook or Staten Island. There must have been a great deal of bewilderment and even some indignation, for much money had been lost, when they bypassed Elizabethtown, the natural leaping-off place for an invasion of Staten Island.

To the high command that was the most anxious time. Washington himself, still with the troops, called a whole day's halt at Springfield to enable the ranks to close, for he had heard reports of a British concentration on Staten Island, and if he was to meet an attack he didn't want it to be in flank and with a column full of holes.

If the British really were massing troops on Staten Island— and the reports might have been true—it was defensively and because they believed as Washington wanted them to believe. When they had seen roads being repaired which could hardly be of any use to the Continental army *except* as routes for an invasion of New York City, the conclusion was natural enough. If for an instant even so sluggish an operator as Sir Henry Clinton knew that his enemy was marching past him in two far-apart bodies complete with baggage and camp followers, assuredly he would have pounced.

All the same, Washington when he called that halt must have been holding his breath.

The Continentals had taken the more easterly of the two routes laid out, and this, of course, was the one nearer to Clinton, the one that would be smashed first if there was an attack. They marched by Paramus, Springfield, Brunswick.

The French, farther west, were treated to some truly *sauvage* country, after which Connecticut, in retrospect, must have seemed prim. The French went from King's Ferry to Kakiate, then Suffern, Pompton, Morristown, Middlebrook. As before, they were fascinated—and the people were fascinated by them. The French were a hit wherever they went. Just for a little while, back in New York State, a few of them had tried a little looting, but the punishments, as inflicted by their own officers, were swift and severe; and there was no more of that.

After Springfield, Washington rode ahead, as did Rochambeau from his column, for they both had business to conduct in Philadelphia. So close was the secrecy that no arrangements had been made for the chartering of boats on the Delaware. Philadelphia, that is, was not expecting these visitors.

After Springfield, too, and when it became clear that they were going south, the men in the Continental column started a somewhat noisy grumbling. The French went where they were told to go, and cried out that it was all *magnifique,* but New

Yorkers and men from New Jersey and Connecticut failed to see why they should be sent all that distance to an unhealthy state. Why couldn't Virginia defend herself? There was no mutiny, but there was not much *esprit de corps* either.

Washington and Rochambeau met and had dinner together at Princeton, and it was just after that meal, and as they were about to start for Trenton, that Washington was handed a report that greatly troubled him.

It was from his favorite lookout[39] on Sandy Hook, and it reported the appearance off that spit of a fleet of eighteen warships, all of them indubitably British.

That was the evening of August 29. The next morning there was another message from the same lookout, somewhat amending the previous one—not eighteen ships of the line but fifteen of those plus four frigates. Even so, if this force—was it Rodney, up from Jamaica? or his second-in-command, Hood?—joined with the fleet Graves commanded in New York, they'd have a force as big as that of De Grasse.

And by the way, where *was* De Grasse? Not a word had been heard of him since he sent by *Concorde* a message to De Barras that he was about to sail from Cap François.[40] Could he have changed his mind? Could he have been trounced by Rodney, a formidable foe? It was not yet the hurricane season, but you never could count on hurricanes. Had De Grasse's fleet been scattered?

Also, what about De Barras? He had sailed from Newport: that much the commander in chief did know. But if De Barras ran into this fleet off Sandy Hook—a fleet that was obviously about to take to the open sea, as his informant had told him—he would be swamped. He would never get to Virginia to bolster De Grasse. He would never deliver that invaluable siege train, or the fifteen hundred barrels of salted meat he was carrying for Rochambeau.

It was a badly worried Washington who rode into Philadelphia September 1, 1781. The news from the following columns was good. The men, the Americans at least, were grumbling;

but they always grumbled, and they were marching fast, as were
the French, as much as twenty-two miles in a day. The news
from Lafayette was good. The news from Nathanael Greene
too was good, in the circumstances. All the same, the commander in chief wished that they'd hear something from
Admiral de Grasse.

There was a great deal to be done in Philadelphia. There
would not be boats enough for any part of the army, barely
enough for the field guns and the heavy supplies. Congress was
in session, as always, and there were certain leaders with whom
the commander in chief had to consult. Word had reached him
that the complaining Continentals, who would soon be entering
this city, had cried that they'd be damned if they would go any
farther than Philadelphia unless and until they were given at
least one month of their back pay, owing for almost a year; so
Washington once more talked with his friend Robert Morris,
who somehow raised the sum, and in gold. There were social
obligations too, what with the Count de Rochambeau and the
distinguished members of his staff in town.

There had been no rain in a week, and Philadelphia sizzled:
it baked in the sun. Nevertheless when the Frenchmen came
they were welcomed with shouts of glee, though it was hard
even to see them for the dust. They put on a parade, of course.
Nobody paid much attention to the poor ragged Continentals,
who, as long as they got that month's back pay, didn't care.

Washington could not get away until the fifth. He would ride
down to Head of Elk, though Rochambeau, because he wished
to have a look at the river fortifications, was taking a barge.

This was not a road of happy memory for George Washington.
The last time he had ridden it south out of Philadelphia was in
this same season, almost on the very same day, four years ago,
when he was to meet Howe on the banks of the Brandywine—
and be badly beaten. Was that significant? Did it mean anything? Were the men back there, his aides, calling this Disaster
Road?

And—what *had* happened to De Grasse?

They had gone only a few miles below Chester when a dusty messenger approached from the other direction, the south. Here was a packet of letters, which Washington opened on the spot, and the very first one was from Admiral François Joseph Paul de Grasse, Marquis de Grasse-Tilly and Comte de Grasse, who begged to inform General Washington that he was anchored in Lynnhaven Bay with twenty-eight ships of the line and a large number of smaller craft, also 3,300 soldiers whom he was now landing, for he had made contact with the Marquis de Lafayette. He was, now, entirely at the service of Monsieur le Général Washington.

Chapter Twenty-four

NOBODY EVER HAD SEEN the commander in chief act like this before. He wheeled about, and galloped back to Chester, where he knew that General Rochambeau's barge soon would put in: he wished to give the good news to his fellow commander in person.

He whipped off his hat when he sighted the approaching general. He windmilled his arms. He shouted at the top of his lungs. And when Rochambeau came ashore George Washington embraced him.

It might have damped his spirits a bit when he got down to Head of Elk and found that not enough shipping was available to move even half of his men, though he scoured the little harbor and the adjoining shores of the bay for fishing smacks, oyster boats, anything he could get.

Baltimore might be able to do better. He would go there.

The news from Heath in the north was good. The British in New York had made no demonstration in his direction.

The latest message about the British fleet was puzzling, and rather disquieting. It had been seen, far out, from a point a little south of Cape Henlopen, the southern lip of Delaware Bay, on September 3, and at that time it appeared to be standing *north*. But this must have been an error. The distance had been great, and the air hazy.

Baltimore went wild about George Washington. Hard though he rode, outstripping aides who were half his age, the news of his coming had somehow preceded him, and he was met by a guard of honor in the outskirts of the city, where there were the usual bonfires and toasts and speeches, Washington reading a speech written for him by Jonathan Trumbull, Jr., a speech much more pompous than any he himself would have composed.

He stayed at the Fountain Inn that night, and early the next morning, the ninth, a Sunday, he was off for Mount Vernon, sixty miles away. He had invited his general officers and their "families" to dinner the following night, and as a good host it behoved him to make preparations. There was no doubt, from the beginning, that he would get there first. The man seemed tireless. Despite the condition of the roads—and he made a note that the militia must be ordered to repair these, since much of the army might have to march over them very soon—he reached Mount Vernon just a little after sunset, which that day was six-twenty.

He had not seen the place in six years and four months, though all that while he had kept up an anxious correspondence about it and its care, for he loved it dearly. He had little enough time to look around now. Everything must be made ready for the visitors. Everything was. When they got there the following night the board groaned. There was no shortage of food at Mount Vernon. There never was.

It was not like that everywhere in Virginia. The troops between the James and the York were hungry. It was the old story of Valley Forge again: There was food, but there were not wagons enough or horses enough to move it. In addition, the weather had been misbehaving.

They had cursed the rain when they moved across the Hudson

at King's Ferry. They would not have cursed it now. Virginia
had been suffering from a drought—weeks without a drop—
so that the streams were so pitifully small that the mills would
not turn, and hence there was no bread for the soldiers, who
lived largely—and most uncomfortably—on green corn.

The generals left Mount Vernon on the twelfth, on the road
to Fredericksburg, and somewhere between Colchester and
Dumfries a messenger appeared with dire news from the sea.

Admiral de Grasse had heard that the British were outside
the capes, and he had sallied forth to meet them. That was a
week ago, and nothing had been heard from or seen of either
fleet since.

Which one would first appear?

If De Grasse was driven off, if the British could carry away
Cornwallis and all his men, then indeed was the Continental
cause lost. Then Washington would have no other place to go
but back to the Hudson River Highlands, and he could hardly
hope to get there with his army intact. Then, almost certainly,
the French, disgusted, would go home.

They put up that night at Fredericksburg, and nobody was
talking much.

British, French, Dutch, and Spanish, all gave great weight to
control of the West Indies, which were thought to be not only
in themselves great sources of wealth but also focal points of
world power. France, defeated, had signed away Canada with
tears of humiliation rather than tears of regret, but she would
cling with the fierceness of a tiger to Guadeloupe and Martinique, while Spain, even when her western empire was crum-
bling around her, never forgave England for the grabbing of
Jamaica. The mainland of North America was not esteemed of
as great consequence, excepting as it might be used as a base
from which to operate to and through the Antilles.

All military and all mercantile thinking stressed the West
Indies. The rest of America was secondary.

Admiral Rodney was an ailing man when the word was

brought to him that Admiral de Grasse, when he headed for the Chesapeake, would take fourteen of the twenty-eight warships he had brought across the sea from Brest. Well, that was no more than natural, in Rodney's reasoning. De Grasse of course would leave the others to protect the French interests in the West Indies; and truly the British must have wondered why De Grasse even told off fourteen for what after all would be little more than a diversion. Therefore Rodney ordered his second-in-command, Sir Samuel Hood, a testy old party who knew his business, to take *fifteen* warships and go north after De Grasse. Then Rodney, pleading ill health, went back to England.

He had been seriously misinformed. De Grasse was anything but a bold, imaginative man, but on this particular occasion he worked fast and hard, and he risked much. He not only took all of his ships north with him for the Virginia capes, but he took along a great treasure and 3,300 troops, all that could be spared from Haiti, as well. If he had done less—or if Rodney had known he was to do as much—history would have been different.

They started at about the same time. Hood, no man to dawdle —and besides, he had copper-bottomed ships—made a direct course from Antigua to the capes, which he reached three days before De Grasse, who, assumedly to escape detection, had taken a much more outside course. Finding no action at the capes, Hood had coasted north to New York, .where he met Graves, who had just returned from cruising off Boston in an effort to intercept a French squadron that in fact never existed: this was not Graves's fault, for he had acted on instructions from Home. These two, then, joined forces off Sandy Hook—it was this juncture that was reported to Washington—and Graves, as senior, took over the command. They had just heard of De Barras's departure from Newport, and they hoped to gobble De Barras first and De Grasse later. Of course, they had no idea of the size of De Grasse's fleet. They started south.

A lookout on Cape Henry sighted the armada at eight o'clock

the morning of September 5, and gave a signal accordingly; and
De Grasse went outside.

He did not have all his vessels, some of which had been told
off to keep the British shipping—including the transports
meant to take Clinton's three thousand reinforcements back to
New York—bottled up in the various small streams that would
not admit these huge warships, and also to patrol the lower
James in such a way that Cornwallis, no matter how alert, would
get no chance to slip off in the direction of North Carolina.
Nevertheless De Grasse had a fine fleet. His flagship, *Ville de
Paris*, a three-decker, carrying 104 guns, was generally regarded
as the best vessel afloat, as it was certainly the largest. He also
had three ships of 80 guns, seventeen 74's, and three 64's, a total,
with the *Ville de Paris*, of twenty-four, all big, all heavy, and
well manned.

The British had nineteen: two 98's (both three-deckers),
twelve 74's, one 70, and four 64's. They had, in addition, four
frigates; but these would not count for much in the kind of
slugging match that impended.

The French had 1,700 guns and about 14,000 men, the
British 1,400 guns and about 13,000 men.

The wind was north-northeast, which gave the British the
weather gauge.

The distance between Cape Charles at the northern side of
the entrance to Chesapeake Bay and Cape Henry at the southern side, is about ten miles. The channel is between Cape Henry
and a shoal known as the Middle Ground, three miles away.
Out through that channel came the French fleet—but it did
not come smartly. Some of the vessels had been obliged to take
a tack or two, or even three, before they could get clear of the
capes. The line was ragged, the van perilously far ahead of the
rest.

Sir Samuel Hood, who always thought that he could do a
thing better than the next man—and was usually right—
declared later that that van should have been chewed to pieces
right then and there. He believed that the "close action" signals

should have been hoisted on Graves's flagship, *London.* But—
Graves was the commander. The signals read "in line."

Battle was joined at four o'clock in the afternoon, and it was
hot and fierce, continuing until a little after sundown. In that
time the leading British ships—some of the others never got
into action at all, a waste—were badly pounded.

Next day, and the next, and the next, as though still panting,
the two fleets just sat and looked at one another. Both sides were
doing whatever refitting they could, in the open sea. Neither
was able to maneuver expertly, being wounded. Some of the
French ships had been hulled, but they were stout. Damage to
the British ships was largely in the standing rigging, which
impaired their sailing qualities, and the *Terrible,* a 74, had been
so badly clawed that on September 10 Graves emptied and
burned her.

Though the British guns, as a whole, still were sound, Graves
never did try to close. As for De Grasse, all he had to do was
stay between the British and the capes, and this he contrived to
do very well.

When at last, September 9, De Barras appeared with eight
more fine French warships, besides the salted meat and the siege
guns—De Barras was late because he had taken a course far
out to sea in order to avoid the fleet from New York—the
British gave up. They limped back to New York. And Admiral
de Grasse returned to Lynnhaven Bay to spread the good news.

This news reached Washington in the French camp at Williamsburg early on the morning of the fifteenth, and it caused
the wildest excitement.

The game was up now. Cornwallis was lost.

On top of all that, it started to rain—and to rain so hard
that soon the mills were turning once more.

Chapter Twenty-five

THE ARMY IN THE Hudson Highlands had been motionless for more than two years, not because of irresolution on the part of its commander but because of lack of supplies, enlistments, money. When the French came, Washington had sent out yet another heartfelt personal call to the individual states for soldiers. The result was a dribble. Some states sent none at all, and one, Massachusetts, didn't even take the trouble to acknowledge receipt of the appeal.

Yet the very existence of this army worried the easily worried Sir Henry Clinton, who at all times feared an attack from the north and so was receptive to any suggestion for scattering Washington's pitiful force or keeping it off-balance.

Benedict Arnold, recalled from Virginia in June, was full, as always, of ideas. He proposed a series of raids on various key points in the "back yard" of the Continental army—Connecticut. Such a policy would cause Washington to send out all sorts of protective forces, decentralizing his army in the Highlands. Arnold proposed himself as leader of these raids. He knew Connecticut well, for he had been born and brought up there. Who better equipped, then, to ravage the state? Clinton listened.

The first raid was to be on New London, where large supplies of food had been stored. When the time for it came, Washington already had split his army and was on his way south with almost half of it, leaving the force at and near West Point even less capable of committing any aggressive act; but it was too late, by then, to change plans, so the venture went off as scheduled.

It was to be a hit-and-run affair, but on a large scale. When Arnold sailed up Long Island Sound to pay the old folks a visit, he had fully 1,700 men under his command. They were a mixed lot, divided into two groups, the first consisting of the British Fortieth and Fiftieth regiments and the Third Battalion of New Jersey Volunteers (loyalists), besides a few field pieces, while the second was made up of the British Thirty-eighth and two "Loyal

American" or Tory battalions. In addition, there was a small detachment of Jägers in each division. These Jägers were what elsewhere in the western world would have been called chasseurs, sharpshooters, tall and terrible men, recruited usually from the ranks of professional hunters and gamekeepers. They had a reputation, in America at least, for ferocity—a reputation the day of September 6, 1781, was to do nothing to erase.

A landing was made at the mouth of the Thames, in order first to take the two forts, Trumbull and Griswold, built on the west bank to protect the river itself. Trumbull was easy, since it had not been built with a land attack in mind and was open in the rear. Griswold was a much tougher nut to crack, being square, with thick stone walls twelve feet high, a ditch, and a determined garrison of almost two hundred men. The commanding officer would have surrendered when called upon to do so, for it was clear that Fort Griswold could do nothing to protect the city against such an invasion as this; but when he was promised reinforcements (which never were sent) he decided to fight awhile. Twice the British, Jägers, and New Jerseyites threw themselves against the place, and both times they were beaten back with heavy losses. The third time they made it. The patriots thereupon threw down their guns, and Lieutenant Colonel William Ledyard, their commanding officer, in token of surrender handed his sword to Colonel Van Buskirk of the New Jersey battalion. Military etiquette would have called for Van Buskirk to hand this back, saying that he could not take the weapon of a man who had used it so valiantly. Van Buskirk had other ideas. He ran Ledyard through the body with the thing. And two soldiers—whether on orders or of their own accord never was made clear—finished the job with bayonets.

What followed can only be accounted for on the ground of battle frenzy. The men had fought hard, the day was hot. In effect, they went crazy. They charged the unarmed patriots with their bayonets, and they chased them to remote corners of the fort, clubbing and goring them, hauling them, screaming, out from under gun carriages, running them through again and again. There were sword wounds too on many of the corpses afterward, so that it can be doubted that the officers did much to restrain or try to control this fit of madness. When it had subsided, the place was a shambles. Where there had been 6 battle dead and 18 wounded, there were now 85 dead and 60 wounded, most of them very seriously. All, living and dead, had been stabbed and hacked with a St. Bartholomew's Day ferocity. Blood was everywhere.

Meanwhile Arnold himself was leading the other division into the city. They were met by insignificant resistance, and they burned and looted right and left, destroying huge supplies of food, capturing several ships and seventy-one cannons, and leaving behind them mostly ashes—and the mangled corpses at Fort Griswold.

The British losses came to 48 dead and 145 wounded, which shocked Sir Henry Clinton, who might also have been shocked by the massacre, though the official report tut-tutted this. It had been too high a price to pay, Clinton decided. There would be no more raids.

That was the last action in the north.

Chapter Twenty-six

TWO DAYS LATER the last battle of the war, properly speaking, was fought far away from New London.

This was at Eutaw Springs, South Carolina, September 8.

The brilliant young Lord Rawdon (his luck had run out, for on the way back Home his vessel was taken by De Grasse and he himself was sent to Brest as a prisoner of war) had been succeeded by Lieutenant Colonel Alexander Stewart, by no means as alert and imaginative a man.

Stewart was encamped at the Springs with about two thousand

men, a tired, hungry, overworked lot, most of them British regulars, though there were a few New York and New Jersey Tories, and of course many deserters. Desertion had been exceptionally heavy on both sides in this campaign for many months. "We fought them with Englishmen and they fought us with Americans," Nathanael Greene liked to say.

Greene had been encamped in the Santee High Hills, a salubrious spot along the east bank of the Wateree, a great treat for his ague-ridden, fever-shaken men. Stewart apparently assumed that he would stay there indefinitely, for he made no adequate preparation against surprise.

He did not know his opponent. Greene was yearning for that one last knock-down-and-drag-out. He had accomplished wonders, for in a few months after taking over a rag of an army, and under the most trying conditions imaginable, he had virtually driven the British out of North Carolina, South Carolina, and Georgia, so that they now held only a few strong seaports —Wilmington, Charleston, Savannah. He had kept them on the jump, puzzled them, worn them down; but though he had battled them many times—with the two patriots' victories, Kings Mountain and Cowpens, Greene was not directly concerned— he had always, while *actually* winning, *technically* lost. The other side invariably had kept the field or captured more field guns—a lot of importance attached to guns as trophies, as though they were some kind of counters to be chalked up on a score board—or both. And Greene did want so badly to win this battle!

He had about 2,400 men with him when he approached Eutaw Springs. Many were militia, but they were not the raw militia of a little while ago, for now they were hardened troops.

The British, out of flour, had been subsisting pretty much on sweet potatoes, and it was a sweet potato "rooting" or foraging party that Green first came upon. This was only a few miles from the British camp, where nothing was suspected.

Yet the surprise did Greene very little good. British discipline prevailed; Stewart deployed his men quickly and well; and the ensuing battle showed no flash of tactical genius, but was long, hot, dusty, dirty, savage, another of those toe-to-toe meetings. The patriot militia behaved magnificently. The British broke, and were pushed clear back through their own camp. Complete victory seemed only a matter of minutes away. It would be a victory hard-won, but it would be thorough. There seemed not the slightest doubt of it.

A detachment of grenadiers and light infantry, about three hundred men, on the British right, hidden in a blackjack thicket, refused to retreat with the others, and now, as the patriots advanced, were enfilading them. Colonel Washington with a sadly depleted company of horse charged that thicket, only to learn that he couldn't get through. That left him and his men exposed to a murderous fire from the retreating British and the men in the thicket alike. Every one of his men was either killed or wounded. Washington himself was knocked off his horse, dragged some distance with his foot still in a stirrup, and bayonetted, before he was taken prisoner.

Now the Maryland and Virginia Continentals in the center of the advancing line found themselves in the very middle of the British camp. The temptation was too much, and they began to loot. There was liquor, and they began to drink. These were the best men Greene had; and the pause, though it might have refreshed, gave the British a chance to catch their breath and to get back together again.

The leader of the valiant little group in the blackjack thicket, a Major Marjoribanks, now ordered a sally. And Stewart had been rallying his men in the rear. The British closed in.

The patriots, who a few minutes ago had been virtually certain of victory, did not break. They fell back in good order, fighting; but they did fall back. The British held the field. Their casualties had been greater than those on the American side, amounting to more than forty per cent (including the hero of the day, Marjoribanks, who died of his wounds), for it was a very bloody battle; but they did hold the field, and they had captured two field pieces to the Americans' one, and therefore they were, officially, the winners.

Greene, his record still unmarred by a single victory, wept with rage.[41]

Congress gave him a gold medal anyway.

Chapter Twenty-seven

WHEN HE HAD STARTED to ride across his native state George Washington was accompanied by a large staff, but what with sending messages right and left, and what with the killing pace he kept up, there were scarcely a dozen of these left when at last he reached Williamsburg. Yet the others were coming, close behind. Many were coming.

Nothing had slipped. Here surely was a triumph of the military art. Almost seventeen thousand troops, besides two separate fleets and a massive siege train, had been caused to converge at a single remote spot most of the men never had seen or even previously heard of, yet there had been virtually no desertions or straggling, and there was very little sickness. Where in Europe, with her vaunted armies, could that accomplishment be matched?

Lord Cornwallis was sealed in. With only Lafayette's skimpy army blocking his exit he might have fought his way away, though he would have been mauled in the process. Even after the 3,300 French soldiers had been landed by De Grasse, and under the command of General Saint-Simon had joined Lafayette, a man of Cornwallis' vigor and skill might have found a hole—or created it. He seems never even to have considered this. He only dug himself in deeper. And now he was doomed.

Why? How did it happen that so clever a general had let himself be clapped into a bag? Only the British navy could save him now, and Cornwallis himself appeared to be becoming at last aware of this fact.

In the past either he had taken the British navy for granted, simply assuming that it would always function as it should, would invariably overawe or if needs be whip the French navy, or else he, an Army man, had merely regarded the navy as a convenience, something that carried supplies or guarded them during carriage, not as a fighting force in itself, a distinct arm of the service. Whatever the reason, Lord Cornwallis was not, so to speak, sea-conscious. Of all the leaders involved in this great movement, he was the only one, on either side, who did not accept the seemingly inescapable fact that nothing notable could be done in this war without control of the coast. He had never hesitated to go far inland, away from his base. Once he even proposed to Sir Henry Clinton that they evacuate New York in order to operate in the Chesapeake Bay region. The sea had been a blind spot in Lord Cornwallis's mind—until now.

Yorktown, the county seat of York County, once had been a flourishing port, a rival of Williamsburg. For one reason or another—the war itself hastened the process—Yorktown had declined to a sleepy village of sixty-odd houses and a few public buildings, including the oldest customhouse.[42] It stood on a bluff on the south bank of the York River about ten miles from the open Chesapeake Bay. The James flowed to the south, making a narrow peninsula, and there were sundry bogs and marsh-lined streams to the north-northwest, the direction of Richmond, which was about sixty miles away.

The York at this point is about two miles across, generally; but another peninsula, Gloucester, with the town of that name at its tip, extends like a pointed finger toward Yorktown only half a mile off. Obviously, then, it would be necessary to seize and to occupy the Gloucester peninsula as well, for otherwise an enemy could mount guns there and bombard Yorktown. Cornwallis sent two of his best officers, Lieutenant Colonel Dundas, a New York loyalist, and the hated Lieutenant Colonel

Tarleton, across to this place. They had about seven hundred men.

Cornwallis himself retained at Yorktown something over six thousand men, including about one thousand sailors from his "navy." This, anchored off Yorktown, consisted of two large frigates, each a 44, *Charon* and *Guadeloupe,* and three transports.

The frigates could not venture into the open bay, for fear of the French, yet neither could the French, with their great drafts, reach the frigates this far up the river.

As for the transports, they had been brought around in order that Cornwallis might use them for sending the three thousand reinforcements Clinton had ordered. Those reinforcements never had been sent. This was not because of De Grasse, but because of Clinton, who kept changing his orders, first directing that the reinforcements be sent to Philadelphia instead of New York, and then, as he began to grasp the seriousness of his second-in-command's position, ordering them not to be sent at all. (By that time Cornwallis could not have sent them anyway, for De Grasse had arrived. Yet Clinton should not be blamed entirely for the quick changes in command, for he had to take *his* orders from the bird-brained Germain, who was still striving to run the war from London.)

Given time, and command of the sea, it would have been an easy matter to starve any army into submission at Yorktown. The allies had command of the sea, but they did not have time. De Grasse had been emphatic about that October 15 deadline. He had only borrowed those 3,300 soldiers, and he had promised to return them to the West Indies before the end of October: so he said. One of the first things that Washington did after reaching Williamsburg was write to De Grasse suggesting an appointment. He meant to ask for more time.

Then he went forth to examine the British outworks.

These were strong. They consisted of seven redoubts and six batteries, and it was clear that they would have to be taken one

PLAN OF THE SIEGE OF YORKTOWN Oct. 1781

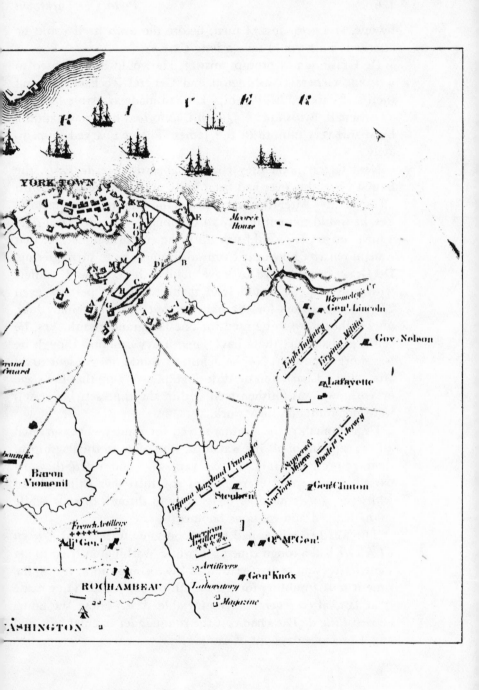

by one, at a great loss of men, before the town itself could be attacked. This would take a long time.

De Grasse sent a prompt answer. He would be delighted to welcome General Washington and General Rochambeau and their staffs aboard his flagship. He had made available to them a fast, small, British prize, *Queen Charlotte,* which was standing by at this very minute in the James. They embarked immediately.

Next day at noon they climbed aboard *Ville de Paris,* the largest vessel that ever had been built, and were welcomed with all formality. After the ceremonies, the admiral was gracious. Yes, he would consent to stay a little longer, if needed. But *only* a little longer. He would stay until the end of October. At that time, no matter how near Cornwallis might be to surrendering, De Grasse would have to leave, taking the borrowed soldiers with him. Yes, he would lend them 1,800 and perhaps even 2,000 of his sailors for the fighting, but not on regular duty, only if they were to be used for one last grand assault. Yes, he could probably let them have some heavy cannons, though he was short of powder. No, he definitely would not consent to an attack upon Charleston or Wilmington, assuming that the siege of Yorktown was finished well within the time set: his vessels were not built for such work.

Urged amiably, the visitors stayed for dinner. They greeted all the captains of all the warships, who came to the flagship in their respective barges. It was very gay; and when they departed that evening every one of the thirty-five ships saluted with every single member of its crew in shrouds or tops, while colors flapped and cannons boomed.

The weather, which had been good, now turned bad. *Queen Charlotte* had a rough time of it, while Washington tried to get some letters and orders written in his rocking cabin, to use the time it took fumbling for the mouth of the James. They made it at last, after several uncomfortable days. Those six hours aboard *Ville de Paris* had cost the commander in chief four and a half precious days out of camp.

News now came from the neighborhood of New York that the expected reinforcements for Clinton had arrived and that they had been accompanied by a fleet under Admiral Digby, a fleet that was variously estimated at from three to ten ships of the line. This did not notably disturb George Washington, a man calloused to rumors; but it did disturb Admiral de Grasse, who now wrote that he was fearful of his position here in the bay and was preparing to go outside and cruise. If he was to meet the British fleet, it ought to be out there. Of course, he might not be able to get back. . . .

Washington, Rochambeau, Lafayette, all of them, wrote to implore the admiral to remain. He at last consented to call a council of his captains and put the matter up to them. Washington waited in an agony of anxiety while this was done.

The next note from the *Ville de Paris* came September 27, and it was all right. Washington exhaled. The captains had advised the admiral to stay, so stay he would.

The day after that, September 28, the combined French and Continental armies marched out of Williamsburg to start the siege of Yorktown.

It was a fine clear day, and sunny.

Chapter Twenty-eight

THE WAY WAS FLAT, for this was low country, scarcely above sea level. The ground was sandy, which meant that it would have to be shored with fascines, gabions, saucissons—a tremendous labor.[43] There were some woods, not many, not thick, and these generally followed the marshy course of the several creeks or brooks—"runs" they were called locally—that cut the peninsula. None of these ravines offered any real obstruction to the march, excepting one, Great Run. This had been bridged, but the British of course had destroyed the bridge. The Continentals halted the first night just short of it, and slept in the open, under the trees, commander in chief and all, for their tents had not yet been brought up.

Next morning they easily gapped Great Run and moved on beyond its protective trees. They came into sight of Yorktown itself then.[44] The previous day only the church steeple, white against a bright blue sky, had been visible. Now the whole church could be seen, and the houses along the main and almost the only street, and particularly the show place, Governor Thomas Nelson's mansion, a landmark. Yorktown like certain other river municipalities located on and under bluffs—Natchez and Vicksburg in Mississippi come immediately to mind—had its residences high, its commercial buildings low, along the waterfront. The approaching Continentals could not see these buildings, nor could they see the shipping that lay in the river. All that they did see looked peaceful enough, though the town was bordered, on that side, away from the river, by a continuous fortification stippled with redoubts and hornworks.

Washington wanted a better look at that inner line of fortifications, and with only a few aides around him he rode forward.

A cannon coughed. There was a blob of grayish smoke. The ball came so close that it splattered dirt over some of them; but Washington, in the classical manner, perfectly natural to him, did not even take the spyglass from his eye.

This heartened the troops, but it disconcerted the aides, who feared that a kidnaping sally might cost them their commander in chief. They persuaded Washington to permit them to send back for a company of musketmen.

A formal siege was a thing never before known in America. Washington had started this war with a siege; but Boston after all had been six and a half years ago, and it had been conducted at long distance, and though successful it was hardly what any European expert would call a real siege. Washington very much wished this one to go off according to rules, properly. He had Steuben and Du Portail to advise him, chiefly, and he had the example of the French on his left. But it would not be the kind of fighting to which the Continentals were accustomed.

The first thing to do was decide where to attack, and this was unanimously agreed upon, for it was plain—the British left, the allies' right. The next thing would be to open a long line of trenches right before the enemy position, which would have to be done under fire, probably at night. This was known as "opening the first parallel." Later the line would be strengthened with redoubts and guns. Later still, when the enemy had been sufficiently battered, a second parallel, farther forward, was to be dug and strengthened, and guns moved up under the protection of this. Here was the accepted, scientific way to conduct a siege.

There might be half a dozen parallels, in a big siege. Two were all that Washington and his advisers planned for the present. Nor did they see any reason why even the first should be started until the artillery, still only a trickle, all had arrived on the peninsula. Meanwhile, though, the men could be put to work, out of range, making breastwork baskets and filling these with soil. Some 1,200 of them were so employed, while 2,800 others guarded them against sudden attack.

There were no mentionable brushes. The British fired a field piece now and then, but they had no occasion to scout, and for the most part they were quiet, except that they often had band concerts, no doubt to keep up their spirits. Like the French, the British regulars had full regimental bands, not simply fife-and-drum corps. They often played "Yankee Doodle," more often still that current favorite, "The World Turned Upside Down." When the wind was right the men who shoveled dirt into baskets could even hear them singing.

Now for the first time since the siege of Boston the artillery had become of primary importance. Cornwallis was outgunned. He had fourteen batteries containing sixty-five pieces, but none was bigger than an 18-pounder. Many had been stripped from and were manned by gunners from the frigate *Charon*.

The French had twenty 24- and 16-pounders and sixteen mortars and howitzers for siege purposes, as well as thirty-two large guns and four howitzers for the field. It was these that De Barras had brought.

The Continentals had—or *would* have, when they were all landed—three iron 24-pounders, twenty iron 18-pounders, and fifteen brass pieces, including two 12-pounders and some 6- and 3-pounders. These had been hauled across New Jersey, put on barges at Trenton, floated down the Delaware to Christina, wagoned across to Head of Elk, and brought down Chesapeake Bay in any craft that might be available. They were taken into the James River and unloaded at a place called Trebel's Landing, and from thence hauled in some fashion—there were almost no wagons—the several miles to the front. All of this called for an extraordinary exertion. It was made the harder, here on the peninsula, because horses were in such short supply. The countryside for miles around was scoured for any sort of beast of burden, but the British had carried off most of what there had been. Ironically, the British at this very time had decided that they could not afford to maintain the horses, which ate too much, and they were systematically slaughtering them, and for sanitary purposes weighting the bodies and throwing them into the river.

On the morning of October 1 the Continentals awoke to find a pleasant surprise. During the night the British had abandoned several outworks on the road to Hampton, the direction of the planned attack, south of the town. These were three redoubts and a redan, and they were especially welcome in that they would have been costly to storm, while the redoubts at least were just as good occupied, for they faced all ways.[45]

This too cheered the troops, though there was an incident in connection with it that had a depressing effect. Colonel Alexander Scammell, a highly popular officer and an efficient one, had gone out to inspect these deserted earthworks, to make sure that there wasn't some trick there. He was surprised by a handful of British dragoons, one of whom shot him in the back, though it must have been obvious that he could not escape. His wound was hastily treated at Yorktown, and then he was released on parole; but nobody believed that he could live.[46]

Washington was not elated by the acquisition of these strong points. He smelled a trick. He feared that Cornwallis was gathering his men together in order to sneak up the York River some night—he had plenty of small boats—and so get away. Washington had previously asked Admiral de Grasse if he wouldn't send a few captured frigates up the river to a point above Yorktown as a precaution against such a sneak-away, and De Grasse had said no. Now Washington asked him again, and again, politely but firmly, the admiral said no; he was afraid of fire rafts.

The truth is that Cornwallis had a great deal of sickness in his camp, and he needed the services of every man he could command. It would have been conventional military practice to make each of those outworks hard to get; but Cornwallis, never a conventional general anyway, was so sure that he would be rescued that he did not see why he should take further losses.

For he had written to his superior: "If you cannot relieve me very soon, you must be prepared to hear the worst,"[47] and Clinton, badly scared, had given up his pet project of an amphibious descent upon Newport—now that he had a navy man he could get along with—and was urging both admirals, Graves and Hood, to do everything in their power to get their battered vessels in shape to sail. The admirals assured him that they would soon be ready. And then Digby's warships had arrived. So Clinton had written to Lord Cornwallis that he would come soon, and in great force. All Cornwallis needed to do was sit tight.

Chapter Twenty-nine

AFTER ARNOLD, BANASTRE Tarleton was the most hated man in the British army. Though for the most part he led Tories, loyalists, he was himself English, being the son of a Liverpool merchant. He had come along to America just for the hell of it, a volunteer without pay, and from the beginning he had shown amazing skill as a leader of mounted troops. He could strike fast and very hard, and he never loafed, and seemingly never even slept. A good part of his work was raids, whirlwind impressment parties, and the burning of houses, stables, barns. He never spared the torch. He had a brusque way too with prisoners, his contempt for whom he never tried to hide. His appearance befitted his evil reputation. He was somewhat under medium height, but brawny, with broad shoulders—built, indeed, somewhat like Benedict Arnold himself. He was still in his twenties. He was dark, florid, handsome in a bold, arrogant way. Everybody was afraid of him.

At Yorktown, Lieutenant Colonel Tarleton was assigned to the protective point across the river, Gloucester. With him were two other lieutenant colonels, Simcoe and Dundas. Dundas was in charge. They had about seven hundred men in all. Facing them were some Virginia militia under Brigadier General Weedon, and the Duc de Lauzun's legion, the whole being under the command of General de Choisy. This containing force greatly outnumbered the defenders.

On October 3 Simcoe and Tarleton went out on a large foraging party, and at the same time De Choisy with his whole command started for the village. It was De Choisy's purpose to pin the British to the very tip of the peninsula, which would make them easier to watch. Neither side, at that time, knew what the other was up to.

De Choisy's advance guard, a company of dragoons under personal command of another dashing young man, the duke, came into one end of a country lane at the very moment when the foraging party's rear guard, under Tarleton, was going out of the other end.

The French raised a shout and charged. Never a man to run from a fight, Tarleton wheeled about and started at them.

There was a spirited to-do in the course of which the two celebrated soldier-Lotharios almost came face to face. Tarleton was knocked from his horse, but he got another and rallied his men. The French fell back a little. Tarleton was about to charge them when a new force came into the field, attracted by the shooting. This was a company of Virginia militia under Lieutenant Colonel John Mercer. They were good men, most of them old soldiers. After a few exchanges, Tarleton, no fool, saw that what he was facing was not an outflung party but the advance of a whole army; and he ordered a retreat.

De Choisy took up that line, which he was to hold for the rest of the siege. There were to be no more foraging parties on *that* peninsula.

It is interesting to speculate what would have happened if Tarleton and the duke had come face to face. The chances are that they would have sabered one another, and then, if it was still possible, have shaken hands. It is even more interesting to speculate what would have happened to Banastre Tarleton if he had fallen into the hands of the militia. The chances are that they would have hanged him.

This brush, an allied victory for such as it was, caused great cheer on the south side of the river, where the dull arduous work of dragging up the guns went on, aided now by a few oxen, strong beasts though maddeningly slow.

The British guns had opened up, firing off and on all day and occasionally even at night. The allies did not reply. There were few casualties.

The night of the sixth had been picked for the opening of the first parallel. A great deal depended upon the weather. The moon was just past full, and if there were no clouds that night, the pick-and-shovel laborers would be treated to a heavy bombardment. The line was to be approximately eight hundred yards from the British inner defenses. It wouldn't be hard to hit at that distance, in moonlight; and until they dug their own the men would have no manner of covering.

The clouds were kind; and though the British did fire sometimes, their balls did little harm, so that by dawn the trench was finished—and the work of bringing the guns up the rest of the way was begun.

In addition to the deserted outworks, the British had three larger, farther-in redoubts. At least two of these and preferably all three would have to be knocked out before the time of the general assault.

One, a star, was on the edge of the river at the extreme left end of the allied line, held by Saint-Simon's men. This was sometimes called the Fusiliers' redoubt.

The other two were at the far end of the line, near the river but southeast of the town rather than northwest, as the star redoubt was. One was five-sided, the other, nearer the river, a square. They were not connected with one another, nor was either connected with the main works. Men stationed in these two redoubts would make much more perilous the work of opening a second parallel, when it came time for this; and they could render a straightforward assault suicide.

October 9, at three o'clock in the afternoon, the allied bombardment began. The French batteries had been ready first, so the French were asked to start it. The Continentals followed soon after, and then both went on.

It was promptly remarked—by Henry Knox himself, among others—that the French fire was much more accurate than that of the Continentals, who however were doing well. This had been expected. The French, after all, had better guns and better powder, and also, probably, better gunners.

There was no shortage of either powder or ball, and from this time on there was no appreciable break in the allied bombardment. They had set out to hit the enemy; and hit him emphatically, assuredly, and repeatedly, they did.

The British bombardment, on the other hand, soon slackened. It was irregular, erratic, and not very effective.

That night the French under Saint-Simon at the left end of the allied arc opened up with hot shot on the two frigates riding at anchor off Yorktown. *Guadeloupe* got under cover of high land on the far shore, but *Charon,* perhaps because she was undermanned, so many of her crew being ashore, was hit—and she went up in flames, a glorious sight but a sight that few of the allied soldiers could see, because of the bluff. Zealous, the gunners at that end of the line also got a couple of the transports.

Now the time had come when those two troublesome redoubts must go. The second parallel could not be dug as long as they were there. The night of the fourteenth was picked, and with the elaborate courtesy that characterized all relations between the two armies it was decided, or perhaps decreed by Washington, that the French should take the left-hand one, the Americans the right.

These redoubts were about a quarter of a mile apart from one another, some 650 yards from the first parallel, and the one on the right, the square one, the one that the Continentals had been assigned to capture, was slightly smaller.

For the French, Major General Vioménil told off a party of about four hundred from the Gâtinois and Royal Deux-Ponts regiments, with Colonel de Deux-Ponts as commander. For the Americans, Lafayette—it was his division, the light infantry—named a like number of men, most of them from New England, though there were a few New Yorkers under the leadership of no less a personage than Lieutenant Alexander Hamilton, who was back in the war, though on field duty, not staff duty. Lafayette appointed his friend and fellow countryman De Gimat to command, but at this Hamilton protested shrilly. He, Hamilton, was officer of the day, he insisted, and therefore it was his right to lead this attack. The point was a delicate one. Lafayette paused. In time he opined that only the commander in chief should give judgment here. Hamilton agreed; and he

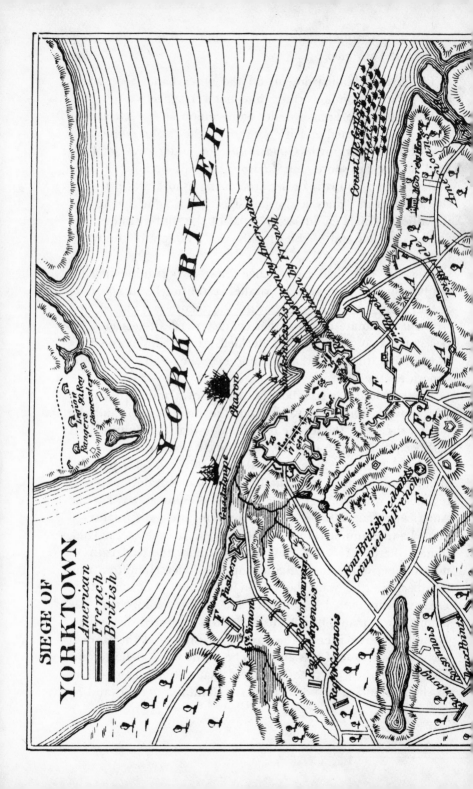

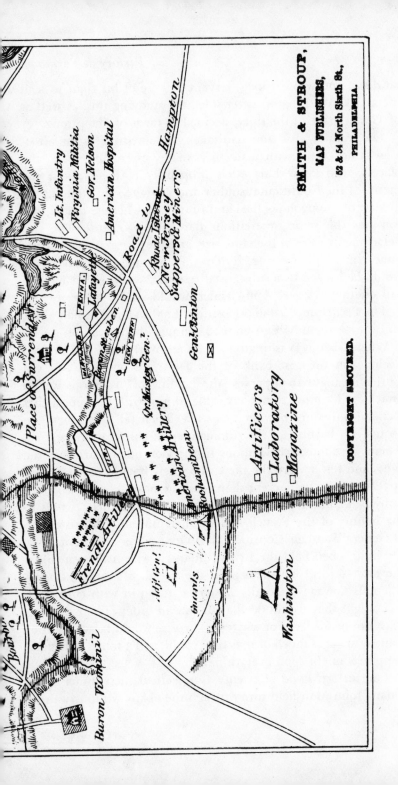

SMITH & STROUP,
MAP PUBLISHERS,
52 & 54 North Sixth St.,
PHILADELPHIA.

COPYRIGHT SECURED.

sat down and wrote a long, fervent defense of his right to lead the attack. Washington, after solemnly studying this, as well as de Gimat's side of the story, decided in favor of Hamilton.

The affair by this time had taken on something of the air of a sporting event, with many bets made, especially among the officers, who knew Lafayette's propensity to boast about the merits of the Continental soldier and knew too that among the loudest of the pooh-poohers and tut-tutters when he talked that way was this same supercilious Baron de Vioménil. The two detachments were of the same size, and they were to start at the same time, side by side. Their missions were similar. Each would be backed by a substantial reserve. Would either have to call on that reserve? And—which would win?

The French met harsh opposition, English and Hessian alike, and it took them half an hour to conquer their redoubt.

When George Washington sat on an overturned and disused beehive on the east bank of the Delaware one bitterly cold Christmas night to supervise the landing of his troops for an attack on Trenton, somebody came to him with the report that General Sullivan's powder was wet. "Then tell the general to go in with bayonets," the commander in chief calmly replied. There were few such weapons in the Continental army at the time, and fewer were the men who knew how to use them for anything more belligerent than roasting meat. The Continental army had come a long way with bayonets since then, thanks to the bounty of the French and the magnificent drillmastership of General Steuben. Continentals no longer were afraid of meeting in an open field the British infantry, who had been called the most skillful bayoneteers in the world. Many of the Continentals nowadays actually *preferred* to go in with cold steel.

Tonight they would do that. It was an order. Their muskets must not be loaded. For whatever surprise would be worth, they wanted to get as much of it as they could, and a touch of trigger-happiness might spoil everything.

The forlorn hope of twenty Connecticut men under Lieutenant John Mansfield tore through the abatis without waiting for sappers to clear it away. They scrambled across the ditch. They climbed the parapets, whooping.

The wall was too high for Alexander Hamilton, a stumpy man, who led the main body in person, but he caused soldiers to lean over and offer him their shoulders, and in this way he mounted, himself whooping. It was over almost before he could get there. The whole thing. It was a fierce fight but a brief one —it had taken only about ten minutes, with Continental losses of nine killed and thirty-one wounded, including De Gimat. The British garrison numbered seventy.

Word of this was sent back by runner to General Lafayette. Lafayette saw or heard by ear that the French still were fighting in *their* redoubt, and he penned a hasty note to the Baron de Vioménil: If M. le Baron needed any help, he, M. le Marquis, would be glad to lend him some Americans.[48]

The next night the second parallel was opened, and inexorably the French and the Continentals moved nearer.

(In New York, the admirals at last had everything ready, and Sir Henry Clinton, who also had had everything ready, poured his men aboard their ships. But the wind would not let them get out of harbor.)

The night of the sixteenth the British sent forth two sorties, one to a French battery, the other to an American battery. The wonder was that this had not been done sooner.

Four French and three American guns were spiked by driving bayonets into the touchholes and breaking them off, but the salliers were easily chased away, a score of them being taken prisoner. A few hours later those same guns were firing again. It had been a gallant gesture, but hardly a telling one.

Cornwallis did not even have luck with the weather. Saint-Simon's artillerists had made daytime communication between Yorktown and Gloucester impossible, or at least damned dangerous; but that same night of the sorties the earl did try to get over there with a fairly considerable body of men, evidently with the thought of making a desperate dash for the north. A storm blew up. None of his boats ever landed on the north shore. They had a hard time even getting back to Yorktown.

The next morning, a fine clear one, a drummer boy mounted the parapet near the hornwork in the British inner defenses. This was about as central a position as he could have picked. They were badly battered, those parapets, for the guns were still going full blast.

Nobody could hear that boy as he beat his drum, but everybody knew what it meant. He was asking for a parley.

The cannons went quiet, small echoes chasing themselves away to rest. And now you could hear the drum.

A red-coated officer stepped forth, with a large white flag.

It was four years, to the day, from the surrender of Burgoyne at Saratoga.

Chapter Thirty

THE OFFICER was met halfway to the allied lines by a Continental officer who carried a bandage. The redcoat asked for General Washington. The Continental replied that the commander in chief was in his headquarters, adding that in order to get there they would have to pass certain installations . . . The redcoat understood, and he graciously gave his permission to be blindfolded.

This precaution taken, he was guided back past both parallels, past the leftmost French battery, and the main American battery, down the Hampton road past a fine big open, roughly oval meadow, past the French hospital, the New York encampment, the Maryland, Virginia, and Pennsylvania encampments on the other side of the road, the American park of artillery, and over a little bridge that spanned the swampy Warwick River. Just short of Rochambeau's headquarters and the nearby

French artillery park, they turned to the left and soon were in the presence of the commander in chief.

He had just finished dictating, to Jonathan Trumbull, Jr., a letter addressed to John Blair of Williamsburg, rector of William and Mary College, in which the commander in chief, obviously in answer to a complaint, apologized for the need of taking over various college buildings as emergency military hospitals. "I am very sorry to say that the Number of our Sick and Wounded are increasing so fast that Room cannot be found for their Cover and Convenience. In these Circumstances I am persuaded . . ." Casualties had not been high: 20 Americans killed and 56 wounded, and of the French 52 killed and 134 wounded. Sickness, however, was rampant. More than 1,400 men in the allied armies were bedridden; and even if there had been room for them in the ordinary forward military hospitals, that would be no place for them, since an attempted breakout on the part of Cornwallis, no matter what its military result, certainly would mean a large influx of stretcher cases.

The visitor handed Washington a letter from Earl Cornwallis.

My lord was laconic:

> SIR,—I propose a cessation of hostilities for twenty-four hours, and that two officers may be appointed by each side, to meet at Mr. Moore's house, to settle terms for the surrender of the posts of York and Glocester.
> I have the honor to be, &c.
> CORNWALLIS.

Twenty-four hours? It was too long! Washington never permitted himself to forget that a British rescue fleet might heave into sight at any minute. He lost no time in replying:

> My Lord: I have had the Honor of receiving Your Lordship's Letter of this date.
> An Ardent Desire to spare the further Effusion of Blood, will readily incline me to listen to such Terms for the

Surrender of your Posts and Garrisons of York and Gloucester, as are admissible.

I wish previously to the Meeting of Commissioners, that
your Lordship's proposals in writing, may be sent to the
American Lines: for which Purpose, a Cessation of Hostilities during two Hours from the Delivery of this Letter
will be granted. I have the Honor etc.

Trumbull had written this letter. John Laurens, always the
busybody, looked it over and changed "Cessation" to "Suspen-
sion." Washington approved, and signed it.

Washington then wrote to Admiral de Grasse, first expressing astonishment that the pilots De Grasse had asked for had
not arrived, and promising to look into this, and then enclos-
ing a copy of Cornwallis's note. He hoped, he said, that Admiral
de Grasse would do them the honor to attend in person the
signing of the surrender agreement, "which will, according to
present appearances shortly take place," or, if this was impossible, at least to be represented.

It was four-thirty o'clock in the afternoon when Cornwallis
replied:

Sir,—I have this moment been honored with your Excellency's letter, dated this day.

The time limited for sending my answer will not admit
of entering into the detail of articles; but the basis of my
proposals will be, that the garrisons of York and Glocester
shall be prisoners of war, with the customary honors; and
for the convenience of the individuals which I have the
honor to command, that the British shall be sent to Britain
and the Germans to Germany, under engagement not to
serve against France, America, or their allies, until released
or regularly exchanged: that all arms and public stores
shall be delivered up to you; but that the usual indulgence
of side-arms to officers, and of retaining private property,
shall be granted to officers and soldiers: And that the in-
terest of several individuals, in civil capacities and connected with us, shall be attended to.

If your excellency thinks that a continuance of the sus-
pension of hostilities will be necessary to transmit your

answer, I shall have no objection to the hour that you may propose.

I have the honor to be, &c.
Cornwallis.

There was no time for further correspondence that day, but Washington, always an early riser, got off a long letter first thing in the morning.

He was specific. The idea of sending the Britishers and Germans home on parole was "inadmissible." The wounded and sick must have their own surgeons and their own medical supplies. Yes, officers would be allowed to keep their side arms, and officers and men alike could keep their private property, provided it was not proven to be loot. As to those "individuals in civil capacities," his lordship had been too vague; and no promise could be made until more detailed information was given.

There was one significant sentence: "The same Honors will be granted to the Surrendering Army as were granted to the Garrison of Charles Town." When Benjamin Lincoln handed over to the British a large Continental army at Charleston, South Carolina, the terms—at least, so it was thought by many in the Continental camp—had been overly severe, even humiliating. Lincoln had been exchanged, and was right here now— was, in fact, Washington's second-in-command. Another who had been present at the dictation of those terms at Charleston was Lieutenant Colonel John Laurens, one of Washington's current secretaries, a young Southerner who was not inclined to forget a slight.

Next morning at the Moore house[49] the commissioners met— Lieutenant Colonel Dundas and Major Ross for the British, Viscount de Noailles, Lafayette's brother-in-law, and John Laurens for the allies. After a secret and long argument—it lasted far into the night—they framed fourteen articles of agreement,[50] all of which were passed by Cornwallis perforce, though Washington disallowed one—Article X, which provided that "Natives or inhabitants of different parts of this country, at present in York or Gloucester are not to be punished on account of having joined the British Army." One of the standing orders in the Continental encampment outside of Yorktown was that any who deserted to the British and were subsequently captured or gave themselves up, were to be hanged.

The next day, October 19—it was the very day that Sir Henry Clinton at last was able to sail with the rescue fleet from New York—the actual surrender took place.

Washington's early message left Cornwallis no choice. The same two-hour deadline was set. Washington had been bringing cannons up all this while, though he had not been firing them. Cornwallis signed, as did his senior naval officer, Thomas Symonds.

A little later, under "Done in the trenches before Yorktown, in Virginia, October 19, 1781," the commander in chief signed "G. Washington," to which Rochambeau added his signature and Barras his, the latter acting for Admiral de Grasse, who was ill.

The thing had been done.

It might be difficult to keep the men orderly in these circumstances. If there was any liquor on either side, assuredly there would be drunkenness. If Continentals or Frenchmen got into Yorktown they would loot, and there would be brawls, quite conceivably an uncontrollable riot. It was for this reason that Washington caused the two principal redoubts in the British inner line—one on each side of the Hampton road—to be given up before the formal ceremony of surrender, which was scheduled for two o'clock in the afternoon. At noon, then, this was done, a force of one hundred French grenadiers taking over one post, an equal American force the other. There was no unpleasantness. These would be, in effect, check-points.

That Hampton road, extending due south from Yorktown, was to be Surrender Avenue. The two victorious armies lined it on either side, the French immaculate in their white gaiters and white coats, in their epaulets and pompons, their braid and gold lace, and opposite to them these magnificent ragamuffins, the men of the Continental Army of the United States of America.

It was a telling moment; and the British did not fail. Promptly at two a general officer in a scarlet coat, a man beautifully mounted, emerged from the town and started down between the two lines of men, past both parallels, past the batteries. It was a ride of about half a mile, and at the end of it, off to this rider's right, was that pleasant oval meadow, lined now by alert French hussars. On the opposite side of the road was a group of French and Continental staff officers, all mounted, rigid, staring straight ahead.

Cornwallis? The men on both sides were asking one another this. The redcoat general did not look like Cornwallis, somehow. He looked too good-natured.

He was in fact Brigadier General Charles O'Hara, a worldly, amiable, accomplished, and brave Irishman, the earl's second-in-command.[51]

O'Hara approached the Count de Rochambeau, who was resplendent with medals and ribbons. He started to offer his sword. Rochambeau with a mere flick of the hand referred him to General Washington, by his side. O'Hara, all unchagrined, introduced himself to General Washington, explaining that he was prepared to make the formal surrender in behalf of his superior officer, Lord Cornwallis, who was ill and who had of course sent his regrets.

This was no way to treat George Washington, a stickler for dignity and for the rights of rank, as Cornwallis ought to have known. Without any expression the commander in chief referred O'Hara to Major General Benjamin Lincoln, *his* second-in-command, who sat in saddle nearby. This gave the impression to those who watched—and there were thousands of them —that Lord Cornwallis' representative was being shunted around.

O'Hara didn't mind. He proffered his sword to General Lincoln, an enormously fat executive who seventeen months earlier had proffered his own sword to Sir Henry Clinton after the fall

of Charleston. Lincoln accepted it, but promptly returned it
with the customary compliment. Lincoln would have done this
anyway, even if it had not been stipulated in Article IV that
officers were to be permitted to keep their side arms.

Lincoln then led the Irishman to the meadow and told him
that the regiments were to come out of town one at a time, with
all their arms and equipment that was carryable. Their bands
could play, but, as had been done at Charleston, their colors
must be cased, not flying. They were to leave those guns and
those stands of colors in the meadow, throwing the guns on the
ground, handing the flags to the officer in charge or to such
person as that officer might designate.

Then an aide arrived from General Washington. Would
General O'Hara do General Washington the great honor of
dining with him tonight at his headquarters? O'Hara bowed,
and said that he would be delighted.

The regiments came out in good order, and on time. A few
of the men were drunk, but none was disorderly, and they were
quiet, grim. The three British regimental bands at least occasionally played "The World Turned Upside Down," for they
would make as much show of spirit as possible. The Hessians
had several bands too.

Some, especially among the Hessians, wept openly when it
came time to put their muskets on the ground, and others
slammed them down hard in the hope of breaking the locks.
All, of course, cursed.

It was not the entire army. A few had had to be left behind
on post, and the sick numbered well over fifteen hundred. The
garrison of Gloucester surrendered at a separate, smaller, and
perhaps not so impressive rite. (In the absence of Dundas,
needed in Yorktown as a commissioner, Tarleton was the commanding officer over there, and he was careful to ask General
de Choisy to keep the Virginia militia far back when he offered
his sword; for he too knew what they would like to do to him.
Choisy obliged.) But there were enough to make a good show.

When the men had gone back to town there was a mountain

of muskets in that meadow, besides eighteen German and six British standards. In addition, and besides the shipping, there were 244 field and siege guns, 75 of them brass. The prisoners totalled 7,247, not counting 840 seamen.

The walk-past had been completed, the claws taken out of a whole army, by the time that General Washington and General O'Hara with a few favored friends sat down to dinner—at the fashionable hour of four.

Chapter Thirty-one

THE CAMPAIGN WAS ENDED, but not the war. Cornwallis's was only one of three British armies in America, and it was the smallest of them. Charleston and New York still were occupied. The Continental army still was, virtually, bankrupt. Washington's greatest worry, as it had been at the time the French alliance was announced in 1778, was that the states would take victory for granted and loll back, letting it slip out of their hands; and his greatest hope was that one more campaign, if put on with vigor, could bring about independence and recognition at last.

He was to be disappointed in this hope. He reinforced Greene, after having had a great deal of difficulty persuading men to go down into the Carolinas, and then returned to the West Point region with the rest of his force. There it was the same story all over again. His most strenuous efforts were called for just to keep the army in existence, to see that it was fed and occasionally paid. Once more he sent a heartfelt plea to all the states; and once more he was ignored. He could not think of making any military move; there was no place for him to go.

The officers muttered, for they were fearful that when peace did come Congress would forget its promises of half pay and free land, and he pleaded with them personally and championed their cause in messages to Congress.

That august body was forced or scared into one more scamper-for-cover—to Princeton this time—when a crowd of regular soldiers mutinied in Lancaster and marched to Philadelphia, where they were joined by others, blockading the Statehouse, shouting threats. This uprising was put down without bloodshed.

Major General Alexander McDougall called Major General William Heath an idiot, and much fuss ensued, including a court martial; but this too was settled without bloodshed.

Alexander Hamilton went into Congress. General Stirling died. Generals Parsons and Glover resigned to go back to work. Only now and then, at scattered intervals, did something happen to testify that war was a nasty business, as, for instance, when young John Laurens, trying to resist a British foraging party at Chehaw Neck, South Carolina, was killed. Yet war's inconveniences were always present: the commander in chief was having trouble with his teeth, but the only skilled dentist anywhere near Newburgh was in New York City, and not to be consulted.[52] And so it went.

The French did send over another fleet, the summer of 1782, but it was scarcely half the size of De Grasse's mighty armada, and it accomplished nothing.

It was no secret that the French were disgusted with the lassitude of their allies and had concluded that the Americans didn't want independence enough to fight for it or work for it.

Negotiators were known to be busy in Paris, and there were plenty of rumors; but not until March 12, 1783, did Joshua Barney of Baltimore, aboard the ship *Washington,* bring over formal news and the official text of the peace treaty. Even that was not final, because of commitments to France being predicated on the making of peace between France and Great Britain. However, this peace did come about, soon afterward, and Congress lost little time in ratifying the treaty, which contained an unqualified acceptance of the sovereignty and independence of the United States of America. The ratification was April 15, but official announcement of it and publication of it was put off until April 19, the eighth anniversary of the day of Lexington and Concord, so that the war could be said to have lasted exactly eight years.

George Washington was permitted to go back to Mount Vernon—for a while.

Lord Germain, secretary of state for the colonies, had protested shrilly when the matter of independence was brought up in the British cabinet. He would never vote for it, he declared. Never! He was quietly given a viscountcy and as quietly dropped out of the cabinet—and history. In all fairness, Congress should have awarded him a medal; for he did as much as any one man to help America win the war.

François Joseph Paul de Grasse was not so fortunate. After the surrender of Cornwallis the admiral refused even to consider a descent upon Charleston or Wilmington. True, his stipulated month of October was not yet up; but he pointed out that he had already stayed longer than he should have, and he sailed off for the West Indies, where he met and was trounced by Hood, and was taken prisoner. Later, exchanged, he wrote a justification of his behavior, and was tried and acquitted by a court martial. Soon afterward he died in Paris, in circumstances that hinted of assassination.

Charles Cornwallis, second earl of Cornwallis, not at all abashed by his surrender, was wined and dined munificently and permitted to return to New York by special frigate. (He was permitted as well to take with him, on a no-questions-asked basis, as many Tories as he wished, in accordance with the surrender articles, so that there were no hangings after the surrender.) His celebrated spat with Sir Henry Clinton had already begun, but he never made a career of it, as the older man did. Cornwallis got himself a Garter, was sent to India as viceroy, took over the military operations there and won a handsome hatful of victories—all, be it noted, in campaigns that did not involve sea power—and upon his return was made a marquis and governor-general of Ireland.

Banastre Tarleton too went far. Back in England, he served for many years in Parliament, published a book critical of Cornwallis but none too friendly toward Clinton either, and had his portrait painted by both Gainsborough and Reynolds. He lived openly, for some time, with the actress Mary Robinson, but this did nothing to hurt his army career, and in time he became a full general. In 1815 he was made a baronet. He lived to be seventy-nine.

Benedict Arnold went to England. He and his wife were received in what were technically known as the best circles, but there was no cordiality in the reception. Arnold occasionally was consulted on American affairs by the king or by cabinet ministers, but he failed to get an army appointment. It was the same with business. He aimed high, characteristically, striving to get himself elected a governor of the East India Company. He never could understand why he was refused. Heartsick, he went to St. John, New Brunswick, where he again engaged in the West Indian trade, making at least a living. After three years of this he returned to London, and he died there in 1801, in bed.

Notes

1. He later became the second secretary of war (General Knox was to be the first). Fort McHenry, the scene of the rockets' red glare and the bombs bursting in air that memorable night of September 12-13, 1814, when Francis Scott Key wrote "The Star-Spangled Banner," was named for him.

2. This house, a handsome one, stood alone, though it was surrounded by fine orchards. It was officially known as Beverly, and had been built by Beverly Robinson, a Virginian born, who married one of the Philipse heiresses. War came, and Robinson tried to stay neutral, but when he was forced to take sides he chose the loyalists, moving to New York City, which was held by the British. There he raised a regiment largely out of acquaintances and servants who had accompanied him. The estate of course was confiscated by the rebel government, and frequently before this it had been occupied by military men. Later it was owned by Henry Brevoort, Washington Irving's ineffable angler, and later still by Hamilton Fish, governor of New York, U. S. senator, and President Grant's secretary of state. It was burned to the ground on St. Patrick's Day of 1892.

3. It was in this action that the Polish patriot, Pulaski, a volunteer on the Continental side, lost his life.

4. Another famous fort was to be named after *him*.

5. Yet Arnold did not do so badly, according to his own lights. The brigadiership was worth about £200 a year, the colonelcy about £450 plus many perquisites of the sort that Benedict Arnold was expert at dredging. His wife, for her splendid efforts in behalf of the Crown, was granted a £500 pension for life, and each of his three sons—two by his first marriage, though none had as yet reached his teens—was given a commission in the British army, sinecures that amounted to about £225 a year (Van Doren, *Secret History*, pp. 385-7). His

161

property was confiscated, but it did not amount to a small fraction of what he declared it to be worth, and if he did get out of a lot of debts they were debts he probably wouldn't have paid anyway.

6. "Turned off" was a common phrase of the time for execution by hanging.

André was buried below the spot where he died. There is a marker there now. And across the river, at the northern end of the village of Tarrytown, is an André monument, a statue of a soldier on a granite pedestal. This is near the spot where John Paulding, David Williams, and Isaac Van Wart captured Major André.

7. One of the soundest authorities is Belcher's *The First American Civil War,* published in 1911 (see SOURCES). Belcher was an Englishman.

8. Davidson, *Propaganda and the American Revolution,* chapter 17. The quotations are from the *Royal Gazette,* published in New York.

9. Later Lord Harcourt.

10. Now *New* Brunswick.

11. The best detailed account of this coup—which often has been romanticized—is to be found in Mackenzie's *Diary,* vol. I, p. 148 ff. Mackenzie, always the best of witnesses, a careful, thorough, unprejudiced man with an exact, military mind, actually seems to have paced off the various distances, and he provided a map of the vicinity.

12. Presently called the Jumel Mansion, a show place, a museum. It had been Washington's headquarters until the fall of Fort Washington and the Laurel Hill redoubt. It is located in the present Roger Morris Park, on the cliff above Edgecomb Avenue between 160th and 162nd streets.

13. For those who would know more about this obscure episode in the history of the Revolution, Van Doren's *Mutiny in January* is recommended. There is also a good chapter on it in Bakeless's *Turncoats, Traitors and Heroes* (see SOURCES). It is scarcely mentioned in most books.

14. These bravos subsequently were awarded, by court order, André's watch, bridle, saddle, and horse, to be divided among themselves and four others of their kind, lookouts.

15. These instructions are in the handwriting of Alexander Hamilton, who still was at headquarters but still seeking a new post.

16. As in fact he did do, later that year. But by that time the American Revolution to all intents and purposes was finished. For Rodney as a tactician, see Mahan, *The Influence of Sea Power upon History, 1600-1783*, p. 499. Fort Royal was the present Fort-de-France.

17. These of course were not all Hessians, though they were all called that. Lowell, in *The Hessian* rates them, all through the Revolution, as follows:

Brunswick	5,723
Hesse-Cassel	16,992
Hesse-Hanau	2,422
Waldeck	1,225
Anspach	1,644
Anhalt-Zerbst	1,160
Total	29,166

See also Kapp and G. W. Greene, in SOURCES.

18. Now Elkton.

19. "It looked as if the sea, in its stubborn preference for British rule, had reached out to get him." Gottschalk, *Lafayette*, III, 202.

20. This belief was widespread. For example, when for a little while the famous bridge at Concord was almost deserted, just after the first brush, a badly wounded redcoat tried to crawl out of the road and onto some grass, and a badly scared boy, scurrying past, saw this and thought that he was about to be shot—so he hit the redcoat on the head with a hatchet. When his companions came back for the man a few minutes later they found him dead, his head a mass of blood. He had died of the

gunshot wound, not the blow on the head, not the cut, which though nasty was not in itself serious; but the rumor was instantly started, and it persisted through the ranks all during that long and terrible day, that the Americans were scalping all prisoners and all corpses—a rumor that undoubtedly had its effect upon the behavior of the men. The Hessians were all solemnly told this same thing, as soon as they had landed, and no doubt most of them went right on believing it.

21. His son was to become even more famous—Robert E. Lee.

22. Actually $12,000,000 and $3,000,000 for the year 1780, but the following year, while France continued to spend the same, the Americans cut their spending to $1,942,465. Sumner, *The Financier and the Finances*, II, pp. 127-33.

23. This correspondence, militarily correct, seldom was acrimonious, then. It became so after the war, when both the principals and many of their friends published books. Each of course blamed the other. This book cannot go into the controversy, fascinating as it was. The reader is referred (in SOURCES) to Clinton, Cornwallis, Tarleton, Oswald, Stevens, Willcox.

24. It is only fair to note that though this quotation has been accepted by historians all down the line, from the most proper to the most popular, nobody ever produced the original. Gottschalk, who hunted hard for it, points out (Appendix II, *Lafayette and the Close of the American Revolution*) that though Lafayette in his memoirs attributed this remark to Cornwallis, there is no proof; that while major generals of twenty-four were not common in the eighteenth century, neither were they unknown; and that nowhere in the known correspondence of either Cornwallis or Clinton is Lafayette referred to lightly or contemptuously. Perhaps this is only one of those things that *ought* to have been written or said.

25. "The notion that French possessions in the West Indies were menaced by a pending English-American coalition played an important part in bringing France into the War of Inde-

pendence." Corwin, *French Policy and the American Alliance of 1778*, p. 142.

26. John Adams was to believe this to his dying day; but Adams always had been a singularly suspicious man. There was no secret clause, and the French honored their part of the treaty scrupulously. It was the United States that tried to make a separate peace.

27. In an effort to get as many men in as possible, as many horses as practical were excluded, and it is interesting to note that the regulations of the French navy then, as to space aboard a ship, rated one horse as the equivalent of ten men. This is somewhat at variance with the *Quarante chevals, huit hommes* of World War I. Three causes can be suggested: (1) it was the navy, not the army; (2) the men carried all their gear, which in this case was tremendous, all-inclusive; and (3) the horses had to be fed throughout a voyage that might last three months.

28. That is, in effect, Mr. America. Brother Jonathan was the predecessor of Uncle Sam, a character that was not concocted until the War of 1812.

29. The grateful legislature soon afterward awarded him for this service "an elegant sword and a pair of pistols."

30. It is the description of his grandson and biographer, Charles Francis Adams.

31. Clinton, *Narrative,* p. 8.

32. He was later to have a real title, Marquis of Hastings, and was to be described as "the ugliest man in England."

33. As is usual even today, figures on both sides, especially as to the numbers engaged and the casualties inflicted, differ. In this one case, however, the authorities are in general agreement. The author has been careful in every description of a battle to consult what might be called the semiofficial British point of view—and very British indeed it is—as expressed by Sir John Fortescue in his monumental *History of the British Army*. Fortescue, by the way, strongly disapproves of Cornwallis's move into Virginia. History, generally, has disapproved.

34. This was John Gunby, of the First Maryland line. He

demanded and got a court martial, which decided that his judgment had been at fault when he marched his men back to re-
form them but agreed that there was not the slightest question
about his efficiency and his personal courage.

35. Cf. Blumenthal, *Women Camp Followers of the American Revolution, passim.*

36. I am indebted for most of these details to the French-in-
America chapter of Lefferts' monumental work on uniforms;
but see also Perkins, Balch.

37. Du Portail had been chief engineer of the Continental
army clear through the war. He was unpopular with the men,
but nobody ever questioned his ability. Later he became a
marshal of France and minister of war. Thrown out by the
French Revolution, he took refuge in the United States. He
started to return to France when Napoleon came into imperial
power, but died at sea.

38. The present Jersey City.

39. This was David Forman, a brigadier general of the New
Jersey militia, a resident of Freehold. Since the British occupied
all of Long Island and Staten Island, besides Manhattan, easily
the best place from which to watch their naval movements in
and out of New York harbor was Sandy Hook. The channel was
not deep in those days, and warships in particular, with their
great draft, always anchored off Sandy Hook to signal for pilots,
or, on the way out, they paused to drop those same pilots, thus
giving an alert man with a glass, a man stationed on Sandy
Hook, a good chance to estimate their strength and to determine
their nationality and perhaps even the flag of their admiral.
Forman was not the only person so posted, but he was one of
the most diligent, and Washington had great faith in him.

40. The present Cap Haitien. It was a much larger city and
a much busier port in the old days, when the French still had it.

41. "Greene's reputation stands firmly on his campaign in
the Carolinas, his luring of Cornwallis into a false position, and
his prompt return upon Camden after the retreat of Cornwallis
to Wilmington. His keen insight into the heart of Cornwallis's

blunders and his skillful use of his guerilla troops are the most notable features of his work, and stamp him as a general of patience, resolution, and profound common sense, qualities which go far towards making a great commander. One gift he seems to have lacked, namely, the faculty of leadership, to which, as well as to bad luck, must be ascribed the fact that he was never victorious in a general action. Washington's ascendancy over his men was remarkable, but Washington had the advantage of being a gentleman. I am aware that this is now supposed to be no advantage; but Washington considered it to be essential to a good officer, and I am content to abide by his opinion. Saving this one small matter, Greene, who was a very noble character, seems to me to stand little if at all lower than Washington as a general in the field." Fortescue, *History of the British Army,* III, pp. 409-10. It is noteworthy that Fortescue, no mean judge, rates as easily the best general on the Continental side—when he *was* on the Continental side—Benedict Arnold.

42. It still stands. It was built some time after 1720 by the collector of customs at Yorktown, Richard Ambler. Restored, it is today the home of the Comte de Grasse Chapter of the Daughters of the American Revolution.

43. A gabion was a basket of whatever material was at hand, wicker being preferred, filled with sand or with dirt. They were clumsy, heavy things. The sandbag has taken their place. The fascine (the political word Fascist comes from it) was a bundle of sticks tied together. A saucisson (French for "sausage") was a large fascine.

44. It was always called, in formal and informal papers alike, York. Posterity, for reasons of its own, has added the "town," the very opposite process to the one that took place on Elizabethtown, New Jersey, a city that long ago shortened its name.

45. A redan was a two-sided breastwork, similar to the flèches or arrowheads that were used at Bunker Hill, and as such could only face one direction. A redoubt, usually much stronger and larger, was completely enclosed, though not roofed. It might be

a square, an octagon, or pentagon, any shape. There is a star redoubt to be seen today at Valley Forge. The ones abandoned on the night of September 30–October 1 outside of Yorktown were square.

46. He died a few days later, at Williamsburg.

47. This was written September 23 and probably reached Clinton no more than a week later; for there were plenty of small, swift dispatch boats breaking the somewhat lumbrous French blockade.

48. The story is apocryphal. If it should be true, then some other officer suggested that note, for the Marquis de Lafayette himself had no sense of humor.

49. It is still standing, one of the features of the Colonial National Historical Park.

50. These "Articles of Capitulation," with their preamble, are to be found in Appendix A.

51. It is remarkable how few staff officers Lord Cornwallis had in his command. O'Hara was his only brigadier, and there were only two colonels (both German), twelve lieutenant colonels, and twelve majors.

52. When, almost a year after the signing of the peace treaty, the British at last did evacuate New York City, November 25, 1783— a local holiday, "Evacuation Day," for many years thought of as highly as July 4—that dentist was the first person Washington sent for.

Appendix A

THE ARTICLES OF CAPITULATION settled between his Excellency General Washington, Commander-in-chief of the combined forces of America and France; his Excellency the Count de Rochambeau, Lieutenant General of the Armies of the King of France, Great Cross of the Royal and Military Order of St. Louis, commanding the auxiliary troops of his Most Christian Majesty in America; and his Excellency the Count de Grasse, Lieutenant General of the Naval Armies of his Most Christian Majesty, Commander-in-chief of the Naval Army of France in the Chesapeake on the one part: And the Right Honorable Earl Cornwallis, Lieutenant General of his Britannic Majesty's force, commanding the garrisons of York and Gloucester; and Thomas Symonds, Esquire, commanding his Britannic Majesty's naval forces in York River, in Virginia, on the other part.

Art. 1. The garrisons of York & Gloucester, including the officers and seamen of his Britannic Majesty's ships, as well as other mariners to surrender themselves prisoners of war to the combined forces of America and France. The land troops to remain prisoners to the United States; the navy to the naval army of his most Christian Majesty.

Art. II. The artillery, guns, accoutrements, military chest, and public stores of every denomination, shall be delivered unimpaired, to the heads of departments appointed to receive them.

Art. III. At twelve o'clock this day the two redoubts on the left bank of York to be delivered; the one to a detachment of American infantry; the other to a detachment of French grenadiers.

The garrison of York will march out to a place to be appointed in front of the posts, at two o'clock precisely, with shouldered arms, colors cased, and drums beating a British or

169

German march. They are then to ground their arms, and return to their encampments, where they will remain until they are dispatched to the places of their destination. Two works on the Gloucester side will be delivered at one o'clock to a detachment of French and American troops appointed to possess them. The garrison will march out at three o'clock in the afternoon; the cavalry with their swords drawn, trumpets sounding; and the infantry in the manner prescribed for the garrison of York. They are likewise to return to their encampments until they can be finally marched off.

Art. IV. Officers are to retain their side arms. Both officers and soldiers to keep their property of every kind and no part of their baggage or papers to be subject to search or inspection. The baggage and papers of officers & soldiers taken during the siege to be likewise preserved for them.

It is understood that any property obviously belonging to the inhabitants of these States, in the possession of the garrison, shall be subject to be reclaimed.

Art. V. The soldiers to be kept in Virginia, Maryland, or Pennsylvania, and as much by regiments as possible, and supplied with the same rations or provisions as are allowed to soldiers in the service of America. A field officer from each nation, to wit, British, Anspach, and Hessian, and other officers on parole in the proportion of one to fifty men, to be allowed to reside near their respective regiments and be witnesses of their treatment; and that their officers may receive and deliver clothing and other necessaries for them; for which passports are to be granted when applied for.

Art. VI. The general, staff & other officers, not employed as mentioned in the articles, and who choose it, to be permitted to go on parole to Europe, to New York, or any other American posts at present in possession of the British forces, at their own option and proper vessels to be granted by the Count de Grasse to carry them under flags of truce to New York within ten days of this date, if possible, and they to reside in a district to be agreed upon hereafter until they embark.

The officers of the civil department of the army and navy to be included in this article. Passports to go by land to those to whom vessels cannot be furnished.

Art. VII. Officers to be allowed to keep soldiers as servants according to the common practice of the service. Servants, not soldiers, are not to be considered as prisoners and are to be allowed to attend to their masters.

Art. VIII. The *Bonetta* sloop of war to be equipped and navigated by its present captain and crew and left entirely at the disposal of Lord Cornwallis from the hour that the capitulation is signed, to receive an aide-de-camp to carry dispatches to Sir Henry Clinton; and such soldiers as he may think proper to send to New York, to be permitted to sail without examination, when his dispatches are ready. His lordship engages on his part that the ship shall be delivered to the order of the Count de Grasse, if she escapes the dangers of the sea; that she shall not carry off any public stores. Any part of the crew that may be deficient on her return, and the soldiers passengers, to be accounted for on her delivery.

Art. IX. The traders are to preserve their property, and to be allowed three months to dispose of or remove them; and those traders are not to be considered as prisoners of war.

The traders will be allowed to dispose of their effects, the allied army having right of preemption. The traders to be considered as prisoners of war upon parole.

Art. X. Natives or inhabitants of different parts of this country, at present in York or Gloucester are not to be punished on account of having joined the British Army.

[*After each of the previous articles Washington had written simply "Granted," but after this one he wrote "This article can not be assented to, being altogether of civil resort."*]

Art. XI. Proper hospitals to be furnished for the sick & wounded. They are to be attended by their own surgeons on parole; and they are to be furnished with medicines & stores from the American hospitals.

The hospitals stores now in York and Gloucester shall be

delivered for the use of the British sick & wounded. Passports will be granted for procuring further supplies from New York as occasion may require; and proper hospitals will be furnished for the sick & wounded of the two garrisons.

Art. XII. Wagons to be furnished to carry the baggage of the officers attending on the soldiers, and to surgeons when travelling on account of the sick, attending the hospitals at public expense.

They are to be furnished if possible.

Art. XIII. The shipping and boats in the two harbors, with all their stores, guns, tackling, and apparel, shall be delivered up in their present state to an officer of the navy appointed to take possession of them, previously unloading the private property part of which had been on board for security during the siege.

Art. XIV. No article of capitulation to be infringed on pretence of reprisals; and if there be any doubtful expressions in it, they are to be interpreted according to the common meaning and acceptation of the words.

Done at York Town in Virginia Oct 19 1781.

CORNWALLIS
THOMAS SYMONDS

Done in the trenches before York Town in Virginia Oct 19 1781.

G. WASHINGTON
LE COMTE DE ROCHAMBEAU
LE COMTE DE BARRAS, EN MON NOM & CELUI
DE COMTE DE GRASSE

Appendix B

IT HAS BEEN SAID that history repeats itself but historians only repeat one another. Authority after authority, including such respectable and even awesome ones as John Fiske and Henry P. Johnston—whose *The Yorktown Campaign and the Surrender of Cornwallis* after almost a hundred years still is one of the soundest of them all—have written that "the British musicians" or "the British band" at the surrender ceremony played "The World Turned Upside Down." Nobody seems to know who started the story, but it has caught the public imagination. Moreover, it might well be true. But certain other facts should be taken into consideration.

There were many bands on the field back of Yorktown that momentous afternoon. Leaving out the various Continental fife-and-drum corps, there were seven complete French regiments, each of which had its own band, and two Anspach and two Hessian regiments, of which the same can safely be said. As to the British proper, there were at least four regimental outfits, the 17th, 23rd, 33rd, and 71st, and probably more (the 43rd, 76th, and 80th were across the river at Gloucester). If they all played "The World Turned Upside Down" all of the time, it must have been nerve-racking, for the tune's a simple one, not to say insipid, and short. It was popular in the British army in the latter part of the eighteenth century, true, but so were scores of other airs. There was no copyright law in those days, and any writer of verse could appropriate any tune he cared to, without acknowledgment, as John Gay did with every number in his phenomenally popular *The Beggar's Opera,* as Francis Scott Key did when he made the London drinking song, "To Anacreon in Heaven" into "The Star-Spangled Banner" by the simple process of putting new words to it. It was a custom of the time, and not looked down upon.

The origin of "The World Turned Upside Down" is lost in the mists of antiquity. Seemingly the thing first appeared as an

173

Irish or English melody called "Derry Down," though that
might have been something else. A little before the Revolution
it was a Jacobite song, "The King Shall Enjoy His Own Again."
In the year 1767 some anonymous rhymster contributed to the
Gentlemen's Magazine, a London publication, verses he called
"The World Turned Upside Down, or, The Old Woman
Taught Wisdom." These purported to be critical of Pitt's
leniency toward the American colonies, but as satire they are
exceedingly thin and they would hardly have proved popular
in the army. They did, however, serve to keep the air itself
alive, and later other, more appropriate verses were put to this
by unknown hands. Many of these later ones were bawdy. Only
a few have survived.

The idea that some sardonic British bandmaster or perhaps
high officer called for the playing of "The World Turned Upside Down" because of its ironical implications might just as
well be laid aside; but of course it won't be.

There is another explanation, and to this author an even less
likely one. Washington had ominously remarked in one of his
cease-fire letters that the surrendering army would be treated
just as the Continental army under Benjamin Lincoln had been
treated at Charleston, where it is certain that the colors had to
be cased and it was reported that the musicians were told that
they must not play British airs. This latter does not make sense.
In the first place, the American fife-and-drum men couldn't
play songs, only rap out marches. In the second place, there
wasn't any American music anyway—or at least, none that the
soldiers would have heard—there were only American adapta-
tions of English airs. Nevertheless it is solemnly set forth that
at the Moore house near Yorktown John Laurens insisted upon
that phrase in Article III that calls for "drums beating a British
or German march" because he wished to repay the British in
kind for the humiliation at Charleston. Nor could the thought
have been to keep the British from playing "Yankee Doodle,"
for the Continental soldiers, though caricatured in this, loved it
and frequently threw it right back at the British. Anyway,

"Yankee Doodle" was not an American but a British song. Frank Moore, *Songs and Ballads of the American Revolution* (Appleton, 1856); John Tasker Howard, *The Music of George Washington's Time* (Washington, 1931); George Everett Hastings, *The Life and Work of Francis Hopkinson* (University of Chicago, 1926); Oscar George Theodore Sonneck, *Report on 'The Star-Spangled Banner,' 'Hail Columbia,' 'America,' 'Yankee Doodle'* (Government Printing Office, 1909); Burton Egbert Stevenson, *Poems of American History* (Houghton Mifflin, 1922).

Appendix C

THE BRITISH TREATED their John André much as the states treated their Nathan Hale, for genuine heroes who were young and attractive, and who were martyrs to boot, were not notably thick in the War of the American Revolution. Long after the dust had settled, André's remains were dug up and taken to England, where they were immured in Westminster Abbey and a memorial erected over them. Since that time—for the temptation was irresistible—there has been a cluster of stories, a whole *class* of stories, that place the aged, hollowed-eyed Benedict Arnold before that memorial. Sometimes the traitor is pictured as simply staring at the memorial, his face drawn in unspeakable anguish; sometimes he is scowling at it, or weeping or even praying before it; and while in some versions of the story this is done in full daylight, in others the wicked old man sneaks into the Abbey after dark.

The truth is that the body was moved and the memorial erected in 1821, by which time Benedict Arnold had been dead for twenty years.

Sources

ALDEN, JOHN AUSTIN. *The American Revolution, 1775-1783.* New York: Harper and Brothers, 1954.

ALDEN, JOHN RICHARD. *The South in the Revolution, 1763-1789.* Baton Rouge, La.: Louisiana State University Press, 1957.

ALLEN, GARDNER W. *A Naval History of the American Revolution.* 2 vols. Boston: Houghton Mifflin Co., 1913.

ANDRE, JOHN. *André's Journal.* 2 vols. Edited by Henry Cabot Lodge. Boston: The Bibliophile Society, 1903.

ARMSTRONG, O. K. *Fifteen Decisive Battles of the United States.* New York: Longmans, Green and Co., 1961.

ARNOLD, ISAAC N. *The Life of Benedict Arnold: His Patriotism and His Treason.* Chicago: Jansen, McClurg and Company, 1880.

BAKELESS, JOHN. *Turncoats, Traitors and Heroes.* Philadelphia: J. B. Lippincott Company, 1959.

BAKER, WILLIAM SPOHN. *Itinerary of General Washington from June 15, 1775, to December 23, 1783.* Philadelphia: J. B. Lippincott Company, 1892.

BALCH, THOMAS. *The French in America During the War of Independence of the United States, 1777-1783.* 2 vols. A translation by Thomas Willing Balch of *Les Français en Amérique Pendant la Guerre de l'Independance des Etats-Unis.* Philadelphia: Porter and Coates, 1891.

BALDWIN, ALICE M. *The New England Clergy and the American Revolution.* Durham, N. C.: Duke University Press, 1928.

BANCROFT, GEORGE. *History of the United States of America.* 6 vols. New York: D. Appleton and Co., 1883.

BAUERMEISTER. See UHLENDORF.

BEDOYERS, MICHAEL DE LA. *George Washington.* Philadelphia: J. B. Lippincott Co., 1935.

BELCHER, HENRY. *The First American Civil War.* 2 vols. London: The Macmillan Company, 1911.

BEMIS, SAMUEL FLAGG. *A Diplomatic History of the United States.* New York: Henry Holt and Co., 1936.

BEMIS, SAMUEL FLAGG. *The Diplomacy of the American Revolution.* New York: D. Appleton-Century Co., 1935.

BEZANSON, ANNE, AND ASSOCIATES. *Prices and Inflation During the*

American Revolution: Pennsylvania, 1770-90. Philadelphia: University of Pennsylvania Press, 1951.

BLUMENTHAL, WALTER HART. *Women Camp Followers of the American Revolution.* Philadelphia: George S. McManus Company, 1952.

BOLTON, CHARLES KNOWLES. *The Private Soldier under Washington.* New York: Charles Scribner's Sons, 1902.

BOTTA, CHARLES. *History of the War of Independence of the United States.* 2 vols. New Haven, Conn.: Whiting, 1837.

BOYD, THOMAS. *Mad Anthony Wayne.* New York: Charles Scribner's Sons 1929.

BROOKS, NOAH. *Henry Knox, a Soldier of the Revolution.* New York: G. P. Putnam's Sons, 1900.

BURNETT, EDMUND C. *The Continental Congress.* New York: The Macmillan Company, 1941.

BURNETT, EDMUND C. (ed.) *Letters of Members of the Continental Congress.* 8 vols. Washington: Carnegie Institute of Washington, 1921-1936.

CALLAHAN, NORTH. *Henry Knox: General Washington's General.* New York: Rinehart and Co., 1958.

CAMPBELL, CHARLES A. "Robinson's House in the Hudson Highlands," *The Magazine of American History,* IV. Chicago and New York: A. and S. Barnes Company, 1880.

CAMPBELL, WILLIAM W. *The Border Warfare of New York during the Revolution; or, The Annals of Tryon County.* New York: Baker and Scribner, 1849.

CARRINGTON, HENRY B. *Battles of the American Revolution, 1775-1781.* New York, Chicago, and New Orleans: A. S. Barnes and Company, 1876.

CARRINGTON, HENRY B. *Washington the Soldier.* New York: Charles Scribner's Sons, 1899.

CHANNING, EDWARD. *A History of the United States.* 6 vols. New York: The Macmillan Company, 1825.

CHINARD, GILBERT (ed.). *George Washington as the French Knew Him.* Princeton, N.J.: Princeton University Press, 1940.

CLARK, DORA MAE. *British Opinion and the American Revolution.* New Haven: Yale University Press, 1930.

CLARK, WILLIAM BELL. *George Washington's Navy.* Baton Rouge: Louisiana State University Press, 1960.

CLINTON, SIR HENRY. *Narrative of Lieutenant-General Sir Henry Clinton, K.B., relative to his Conduct during Part of his Command of the King's Troops in North America, particularly that*

which respects the unfortunate issue of the Campaign of 1781.
London: J. Debrett, 1783.

CLOS, JEAN HENRI. *The Glory of Yorktown.* Yorktown, Va.: York-town Historical Society, 1924.

CORNWALLIS, EARL. *An Answer to that Part of the Narrative of Lieutenant-General Sir Henry Clinton, K.B., which relates to the Conduct of Lieutenant-General Earl Cornwallis during the Campaign in North-America in the Year of 1781.* London: J. Debrett, 1783.

CORWIN, EDWARD S. *French Policy and the American Alliance of 1778.* Princeton: Princeton University Press, 1916.

CUNLIFFE, MARCUS. *George Washington: Man and Monument.* Boston: Little, Brown and Company, 1958.

CURTIS, E. E. *The British Army in the American Revolution.* New Haven: Yale University Press, 1926.

DALSEME, RENE. *Beaumarchais, 1732-1799.* New York: G. P. Putnam's Sons, 1929.

DAVIDSON, PHILIP. *Propaganda and the American Revolution, 1763-1783.* Chapel Hill: The University of North Carolina Press, 1941.

DAVIS, RICH DEWEY. *Financial History of the United States.* New York: Longmans, Green and Co., 1925.

DAWSON, HENRY BARTON. *Battles of the United States by Sea and Land,* 2 vols. New York: Johnson, Fry and Co., 1858.

DAWSON, HENRY BARTON (ed.). *New York City during the American Revolution: a Collection of Original Papers.* New York: Mercantile Library Association, 1861.

DOYLE, JOSEPH B. *Frederick William von Steuben and the American Revolution.* Steubenville, Ohio: The H. C. Cook Co., 1913.

DRAKE, FRANCIS SAMUEL. *Life and Correspondence of Henry Knox.* Boston: S. G. Drake, 1873.

ECKENRODE, HAMILTON JAMES. *The Revolution in Virginia.* Boston: Houghton Mifflin Company, 1916.

EINSTEIN, CAVIS. *Divided Loyalties: Americans in England during the War of Independence.* London: Cobden-Sanderson, 1933.

EMMONS, G. F. *The Navy of the United States, 1775-1783.* Washington, 1783.

ESPOSITO, COL. VINCENT J. (ed.). *The West Point Atlas of American Wars.* New York: Frederick A. Praeger, 1959.

FISHER, SYDNEY GEORGE. *The Struggle for American Independence.* 2 vols. Philadelphia: J. B. Lippincott Company, 1908.

FISK, JOHN. *The American Revolution.* 2 vols. Boston: Houghton Mifflin Company, 1891.

FITZPATRICK, JOHN CLEMENT. *George Washington Himself: A Common-Sense Biography Written from his Manuscripts.* Indianapolis: Bobbs, Merrill Company, 1933.

FITZPATRICK, JOHN CLEMENT. *The Spirit of the Revolution: New Light from Some of the Original Sources of American History.* Boston: Houghton Mifflin Company, 1924.

FITZPATRICK, JOHN CLEMENT. See also WASHINGTON, GEORGE.

FLEXNER, JAMES THOMAS. *The Traitor and the Spy: Benedict Arnold and John André.* New York: Harcourt, Brace and Company, 1953.

FLICK, ALEXANDER CLARENCE. *Loyalism in New York during the American Revolution.* New York: Columbia University Press, 1901.

FORD, HENRY JONES. *Washington and his Colleagues.* New Haven: Yale University Press, 1921.

FORD, PAUL LEICESTER. *The True George Washington.* Philadelphia: J. B. Lippincott Company, 1896.

FORTESCUE, JOHN W. *History of the British Army.* 10 vols. New York: The Macmillan Company, 1899-1920.

FREEMAN, DOUGLAS SOUTHALL. *George Washington: a Biography.* 6 vols. New York: Charles Scribner's Sons, 1948-1954.

FROTHINGHAM, RICHARD. *The Rise of the Republic of the United States.* Boston: Little, Brown and Company, 1910.

FROTHINGHAM, THOMAS G. *Washington: Commander in Chief.* Boston: Houghton Mifflin Company, 1930.

FULLER, J. F. C. *Decisive Battles of the U.S.A.* New York: Thomas Yoseloff, 1942.

GALLATIN, GASPARD DE. *Journal of the Siege of York-Town.* Washington: Government Printing Office, 1911.

GANOE, WILLIAM ADDLEMAN. *The History of the United States Army.* New York and London: D. Appleton-Century Company, 1943.

GOTTSCHALK, LOUIS. *Lafayette and the Close of the American Revolution.* Chicago: University of Chicago Press, 1942.

GRAHAM, JAMES. *The Life of General Daniel Morgan, of the Virginia Line of the Army of the United States.* New York: Derby and Jackson, 1856.

GREENE, FRANCIS VINTON. *General Greene.* New York: D. Appleton and Company, 1893.

GREENE, GEORGE WASHINGTON. *The German Element in the War of American Independence.* New York: Hurd and Houghton, 1876.

GREENE, GEORGE WASHINGTON. *The Life of Nathanael Greene, Major-General in the Army of the Revolution.* 3 vols. New York: G. P. Putnam and Son, 1867 (Vol. I); Hurd and Houghton, 1871 (Vols. II and III).

HATCH, LOUIS CLINTON. *The Administration of the American Revolutionary Army.* New York: Longmans, Green and Company, 1904.

HENDRICK, BURTON J. *The Lees of Virginia: Biography of a Family.* Boston: Little, Brown and Company, 1941.

HILDRETH, RICHARD. *The History of the United States of America.* 3 vols. New York: Harper and Brothers, 1851-2.

HOWARD, JOHN TASKER. *The Music of George Washington's Time.* Washington: United States George Washington Bicentennial Commission, 1931.

HUGHES, RUPERT. *George Washington.* 3 vols. New York: William Morrow and Company, 1930.

HUNT, WILLIAM. *The [political] History of England from the Accession of George III to the Close of Pitt's First Administration.* London: Longmans, Green, and Company, 1905.

JAMES, WILLIAM DOBEIN. *A Sketch of the Life of Brig. Gen. Francis Marion.* Marietta, Ga.: Continental Book Company, 1948.

JOHNSON, WILLIAM. *Sketches of the Life and Correspondence of Nathanael Greene, Major General of the Armies of the United States in the War of the Revolution.* 2 vols. Charleston, S.C.: Published by the author, 1822.

JOHNSTON, HENRY P. *The Yorktown Campaign and the Surrender of Cornwallis, 1781.* New York: Harper and Brothers. 1881.

KAPP, FRIEDRICH. *The Life of Frederick William von Steuben, Major General in the Revolutionary Army.* New York: Mason Brothers, 1859.

KAPP, FRIEDRICH. *The Life of John Kalb, Major-General in the Revolutionary Army.* New York: Henry Holt and Company, 1884.

KITE, ELIZABETH S. *Beaumarchais and the War of American Independence.* 2 vols. Boston: Richard G. Badger, 1918.

KITE, ELIZABETH S. *Brigadier-General Louis Lebegue Duportail, Commandant of Engineers in the Continental Army, 1777-1783.* Baltimore: The Johns Hopkins Press, 1933.

KNOLLENBERG, BERNHARD. *Washington and the Revolution: a Reappraisal.* New York: The Macmillan Company, 1940.

KNOX, DUDLEY W. *The Naval Genius of George Washington.* Boston: Houghton Mifflin Company, 1932.

LANDERS, H. L. *The Battle of Camden, South Carolina.* Washington: Government Printing Office, 1929.

LECKY, W. E. H. *History of England in the Eighteenth Century.* 8 vols. London: Longmans, Green and Company, 1878-1890.

LEFFERTS, CHARLES W. *Uniforms of the American, British, French, and German Armies in the War of the American Revolution, 1775-1783,* ed. Alexander J. Wall. New York: The New-York Historical Society, 1926.

LODGE, HENRY CABOT. See ANDRE, JOHN.

LOWELL, EDWARD J. *The Hessian and Other German Auxiliaries of Great Britain in the Revolutionary War.* New York: Harper and Brothers, 1903.

MACKENZIE, FREDERICK. *Diary of Frederick Mackenzie.* 2 vols. Cambridge, Mass.: Harvard University Press, 1930.

MACLAY, EDGAR STANTON. *A History of American Privateers.* New York and London: D. Appleton and Company, 1924.

MACLAY, EDGAR STANTON. *The History of the Navy, from 1775 to 1894.* 3 vols. New York: D. Appleton and Company, 1895.

MAHAN, ALBERT THAYER. *The Influence of Sea Power upon History, 1660-1783.* Boston: Little, Brown and Company, 1894.

MAHAN, ALBERT THAYER. *The Major Operations of the Navies in the War of American Independence.* London: Sampson Low, Marston and Company, Ltd., 1913.

MARTIN, LOUIS. *George Washington.* New York: Thomas Y. Crowell Co., 1932.

MILLER, HUNTER (ed.). *Treaties and Other International Acts of the United States of America.* 8 vols. Washington: Government Printing Office, 1931.

MONTROSS, LYNN. *Rag, Tag and Bobtail: The Story of the Continental Army.* New York: Harper and Brothers, 1952.

MOORE, FRANK. *Songs and Ballads of the American Revolution.* New York: D. Appleton and Company, 1856.

NELSON, WILLIAM. "The Traditional and the Real Washington," *The Magazine of American History,* Vol. III, Part II. New York and Chicago: A. S. Barnes and Company, 1879.

NETTELS, CURTIS P. *George Washington and American Independence.* Boston: Little, Brown and Company, 1951.

NEVINS, ALLAN. *The American States During and After the Revolution, 1775-1789.* New York: The Macmillan Company, 1927.

NILES, BLAIR. *The James.* New York: Farrar and Rinehart, Inc., 1939.

OSWALD, RICHARD. *Memorandum on the Folly of Invading Virginia, etc.* Charlottesville: University of Virginia Press, 1953.

OTIS, SCHUYLER (ed.). *The Yorktown Sesquicentennial: Proceedings of the United States Yorktown Sesquicentennial Commission.* Washington: Government Printing Office, 1932.

PALMER, JOHN MCAULEY. *General von Steuben.* New Haven: Yale University Press, 1937.

PECKHAM, HOWARD H. *The War for Independence: A Military History.* Chicago: University of Chicago Press, 1958.

PENNYPACKER, MORTON. *General Washington's Spies on Long Island and in New York.* Brooklyn: The Long Island Historical Society, 1939.

PERKINS, JAMES BRECK. *France in the American Revolution.* Boston: Houghton Mifflin Company, 1911.

PLATT, FLETCHER. *The Navy, a History.* Garden City, N.Y.: Doubleday, Doran and Company, 1938.

PRESTON, JOHN HYDE. *A Gentleman Rebel: The Exploits of Anthony Wayne.* New York: Farrar and Rinehart Inc., 1930.

RICHESON, CHARLES R. *British Politics and the American Revolution.* Norman, Okla.: University of Oklahoma Press, 1954.

ROBSON, ERIC. *The American Revolution in its Political and Military Aspects, 1763-1783.* London: The Batchworth Press, 1955.

RUSSELL, CARL P. *Guns on the Early Frontiers: A History of Firearms from Colonial Times through the Years of the Western Fur Trade.* Berkeley and Los Angeles: University of California Press, 1957.

SABINE, LORENZO. *Biographical Sketches of Loyalists of the American Revolution.* 2 vols. Boston: Little, Brown and Company, 1864.

SARGENT, WINTHROP. *The Life and Career of Major André, Adjutant-General of the British Army in America.* Boston: Ticknor and Fields, 1861.

SAWYER, JOSEPH DILLAWAY. *Washington.* 2 vols. New York: The Macmillan Company, 1927.

SCHACHNER, NATHAN. *Alexander Hamilton.* New York: D. Appleton-Century Company, 1946.

SCHACHNER, NATHAN. *Thomas Jefferson: A Biography.* 2 vols. New York: Appleton-Century-Crofts, Inc., 1951.

SCHEER, GEORGE F., and RANKIN, HUGH F. *Rebels and Redcoats.* Cleveland and New York: The World Publishing Company, 1957.

SCHLESINGER, ARTHUR MEIER. *The Colonial Merchants and the American Revolution.* New York: The Facsimile Library, 1939.

SELLERS, CHARLES COLEMAN. *Benedict Arnold, The Proud Warrior.* New York: Minton, Balch and Company, 1930.

SIMMS, WILLIAM G. *The Life of Nathanael Greene, Major-General in the Army of the Revolution.* Philadelphia: Leary and Getz, 1849.

SPARKS, JARED. *The Life and Treason of Benedict Arnold.* New York: Harper and Brothers, 1848.

SPEARS, JOHN R. *Anthony Wayne, Sometimes called "Mad Anthony."* New York: D. Appleton and Company, 1903.

STEDMAN, CHARLES. *The History of the Origin, Progress, and Termination of the American War.* 2 vols. London: Printed for the author, 1794.

STEELE, MATTHEW F. *American Campaigns.* 2 vols. Washington: Byron S. Adams, 1909.

STEVENS, BENJAMIN FRANKLIN (ed.). *The Clinton-Cornwallis Controversy.* 2 vols. London, 1888.

STEVENS, JOHN AUSTIN. "Benedict Arnold and His Apologist," *The Magazine of American History,* LV. Chicago and New York: A. S. Barnes and Company, 1880.

STEVENS, JOHN AUSTIN. "The French in Rhode Island," *The Magazine of American History,* Vol. III, Part II, New York and Chicago: A. S. Barnes and Company, 1879.

STEVENS, JOHN AUSTIN. "The Operations of the Allied Armies before New York, 1781," *The Magazine of American History,* IV. New York and Chicago: A. S. Barnes and Company, 1880.

STOCKBRIDGE, J. C. "The Case of Major André," *The Magazine of American History,* Vol. III, Part II. New York and Chicago: A. S. Barnes and Company, 1879.

SUMNER, CHARLES GRAHAM. *The Financier and the Finances of the American Revolution.* 2 vols. New York: Dodd, Mead and Company, 1891.

TARLETON, BANASTRE. *A History of the Campaigns of 1780 and 1781, in the Southern Provinces of North America.* London: T. Cadell, 1787.

THACHER, JAMES. *Military Journal during the American Revolutionary War.* Boston: Richardson and Lord, 1823.

THAYER, WILLIAM ROSCOE. *George Washington.* Boston: Houghton Mifflin Company, 1922.

TOWER, CHARLEMAGNE. *The Marquis de la Fayette in the American Revolution.* 2 vols. Philadelphia: J. B. Lippincott Company, 1901.

TREVELYAN, GEORGE OTTO. *The American Revolution.* 6 vols. London: Longmans, Green and Company, 1905.

TYLER, MOSES COIT. *The Literary History of the American Revolution.* 2 vols. New York: G. P. Putnam's Sons, 1897.

UHLENDORF, BERNHARD A. (ed.). *Revolution in America: Confidential Letters and Journals, 1776-1784, of Adjutant General Major Bauermeister of the Hessian Forces.* New Brunswick, N.J.: Rutgers University Press, 1957.

VAN DOREN, CARL. *Mutiny in January: The Story of a Crisis in the Continental Army now for the first time fully told from many hitherto unknown or neglected sources both American and British.* New York: The Viking Press, 1943.

VAN DOREN, CARL. *Secret History of the American Revolution.* New York: The Viking Press, 1941.

VAN TYNE, CLAUDE HALSTEAD. *The American Revolution.* New York: Harper and Brothers, 1905.

VAN TYNE, CLAUDE HALSTEAD. *England and America, Rivals in the American Revolution.* Cambridge: Cambridge University Press, 1929.

VAN TYNE, CLAUDE HALSTEAD. *The Loyalists in the American Revolution.* New York: Peter Smith, 1929.

VAN TYNE, CLAUDE HALSTEAD. *The War of Independence: American Phase.* Boston: Houghton Mifflin Company, 1929.

WALLACE, WILLARD M. *Traitorous Hero: The Life and Fortunes of Benedict Arnold.* New York: Harper and Brothers, 1954.

WASHINGTON, GEORGE. *The Writings of George Washington,* ed. by John C. Fitzpatrick, Vols. XX, XXI. Washington: United States Government Printing Office, 1937-38.

WECTER, DIXON. *The Hero in America: a Chronicle of Hero-Worship.* New York: Charles Scribner's Sons, 1941.

WHARTON, FRANCIS (ed.). *Revolutionary Correspondence of the United States.* 6 vols. Washington: Government Printing Office, 1889.

WHITLOCK, BRAND. *LaFayette.* 2 vols. New York: D. Appleton and Company, 1929.

WILD, EBENEZER. "Journal, 1776-1781," *Proceedings of the Massachusetts Historical Society,* Ser. 2, Vol. VI, October, 1890.

WILKINSON, JAMES. *Memoirs of My Own Time.* 3 vols. Philadelphia: Abraham Small, 1816.

WILLCOX, WILLIAM B. "The British Road to Yorktown: A Study in Divided Command," *American Historical Review,* LII, October, 1946.

WILLCOX, WILLIAM B. "Rhode Island in British Strategy, 1780-1781," *American Historical Review,* XVII, December, 1945.

WILSTACH, PAUL. *Tidewater Virginia.* Indianapolis: Bobbs, Merrill Company, 1929.

WOODWARD, WILLIAM E. *George Washington: The Image and the Man.* New York: Boni and Liveright, 1926.

WOODWARD, WILLIAM E. *Lafayette.* New York: Farrar and Rinehart, Inc., 1938.

WRIGHT, MARCUS J. "Lafayette's Campaign in Virginia, April-October, 1781," *Publications of the Southern History Association,* IX, 1905.

WRONG, GEORGE M. *Washington and His Comrades in Arms.* New Haven: Yale University Press, 1921.

Index